Janice VanCleave's

201

Awesome,
Magical,
Bizarre,
& Incredible
Experiments

Janice VanCleave's

201

Awesome, Magical, Bizarre, & Incredible Experiments

John Wiley & Sons, Inc.

New York · Chichester · Brisbane · Toronto · Singapore

This book is dedicated to three special people who have given me much encouragement—to my friends, Jim, Nancy, and Matthew Land

This text is printed on acid-free paper.

Copyright 1994 by John Wiley & Sons, Inc.

All rights reserved. Published simultaneously in Canada.

Reproduction or translation of any part of this work beyond that permitted by Section 107 or 108 of the 1976 United States Copyright Act without the permission of the copyright owner is unlawful. Requests for permission or further information should be addressed to the Permissions Department, John Wiley & Sons, Inc.

The publisher and the author have made every reasonable effort to insure that the experiments and activities in this book are safe when conducted as instructed but assume no responsibility for any damage caused or sustained while performing the experiments or activities in this book. Parents, guardians, and/or teachers should supervise young readers who undertake the experiments and activities in this book.

Library of Congress Cataloging-in-Publication Data:

VanCleave, Janice.
    Janice VanCleave's 201 awesome, magical, bizarre, and incredible experiments / by
Janice VanCleave.
        p.   cm.
    Includes index.
    ISBN 0-471-31011-5 (pbk. : alk. paper)
    1. Science—Experiments—Juvenile literature. [1. Science—
Experiments.   2. Scientific recreations.   3. Experiments.]
I. Title.   II. Title: Two hundred and one awesome, magical, bizarre, and
incredible experiments.
Q164.V367   1994
507.8—dc20   93-29807

Printed in the United States of America

10 9 8 7 6 5 4

Introduction

This book is a collection of science experiments designed to show you that science is more than a list of facts—science is fun! The 201 experiments in the book take science out of the laboratory and put it into your daily life.

Science is a way of solving problems and discovering why things happen the way they do. How does a battery work? Why is Venus so hot? How can a frog build a nest in a tree? You'll find the answers to these and many other questions by doing the experiments in this book.

The experiments cover five different fields of science:

- **Astronomy** The study of the planet we live on—Earth—and all our neighbors in space.
- **Biology** The study of the way living organisms behave and interact.
- **Chemistry** The study of the way materials are put together and their behavior under different conditions.
- **Earth Science** The study of the unique habitat that all known living creatures share—the Earth.
- **Physics** The study of energy and matter and the relationship between them.

The Experiments

Scientists identify a problem, or an event, and seek solutions, or explanations, through research and experimentation. A goal of this book is to guide you through the steps necessary to successfully complete a science experiment and to teach you the best method of solving problems and discovering answers.

1. **Purpose:** The basic goals for the experiment.
2. **Materials:** A list of necessary supplies.
3. **Procedure:** Step-by-step instructions on how to perform the experiment.
4. **Results:** An explanation stating exactly what is expected to happen. This is an immediate learning tool. If the expected results are achieved, the experimenter has an immediate positive reinforcement. An error is also quickly recognized, and the need to start over or make corrections is readily apparent.
5. **Why?** An explanation of why the results were achieved is described in terms that are understandable to the reader who may not be familiar with scientific terms. When a new term is introduced and explained, it appears in **bold** type; these terms can also be found in the Glossary.

You will be rewarded with successful experiments if you read an experiment carefully, follow each step in order, and do not substitute materials.

General Instructions

1. **Read first**. Read each experiment completely before starting.
2. **Collect needed supplies**. You will experience less frustration and more fun if all the necessary materials for the experiments are ready for instant use. You lose your train of thought when you have to stop and search for supplies.
3. **Experiment**. Follow each step very carefully, never skip steps, and do not add your own. Safety is of the utmost importance, and by reading the experiment before starting, then following the instructions exactly, you can feel confident that no unexpected results will occur.
4. **Observe**. If your results are not the same as described in the experiment, carefully read the instructions, and start over from the first step.

Measurements

Measuring quantities described in this book are intended to be those commonly used in every kitchen. When specific amounts are given, you need to use a measuring instrument closest to the described amount. The quantities listed are not critical, and a variation of very small amounts more or less will not alter the results. Approximate metric equivalents are given in parentheses.

Contents

I
Astronomy

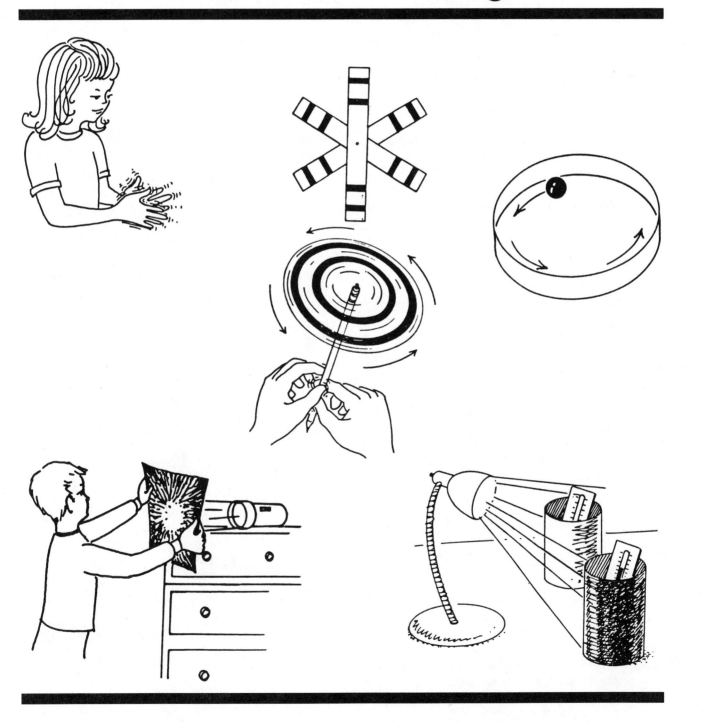

1. Cooler

Purpose To determine how color affects a planet's surface temperature.

Materials scissors
  construction paper (1 piece white and 1 piece black)
  2 empty, metal, food cans, same size
    CAUTION: *Be sure rims are not jagged. They might cut your hands.*
  transparent tape
  2 thermometers
  ruler
  desk lamp

Procedure

■ Cut the white and black construction paper to fit around the outside of the cans, much as the can label does.
■ Secure one piece of paper to each can with tape.
■ Place one thermometer inside each can.
■ Read and record the temperature on both thermometers.
■ Position both cans about 12 inches (30 cm) from the lamp.
■ Turn the lamp on.

■ Read and record the temperature on both thermometers after 10 minutes.

Results The temperature is much higher in the can covered with black paper.

Why? The dark paper absorbs more light waves than the white paper. The white paper is cooler because it reflects more of the light waves than the black paper. The absorption of the light waves increases the temperature of a material. In the same way, the lighter the surface material on a planet, the less light energy the planet's surface absorbs and the cooler is its surface.

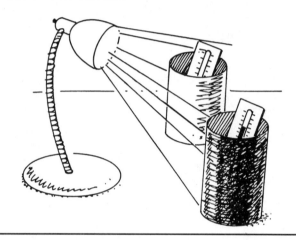

2. Shaded

Purpose To demonstrate how a planet's surface temperature can vary.

Materials 2 thermometers

Procedure

■ Read and record the temperature on both thermometers.
■ Place one thermometer on the ground in the shade of a tree or other large structure.
■ Place the second thermometer on the ground, but in direct sunlight.
NOTE: *It is important that both thermometers be placed on the same type of surface (grass works well).*
■ Read and record the temperature on both thermometers after 20 minutes.

Results The temperature on the surface in the shade is lower than the same surface in direct sunlight.

Why? The tree or large structure blocks some of the light rays, producing a shaded area on the ground. This protected surface area is cooler due to the decrease in light energy received. The same type of surface in direct sunlight receives more light energy and becomes hotter. In the same way, the temperature of planet surfaces can vary depending on whether the landscape has large structures to provide shade.

3. Cover Up

Purpose To determine why Mercury does not cause an eclipse.

Materials desk lamp

Procedure
- Stand about 2 yards (2 m) from the desk lamp.
- Close your right eye.
- Hold your left thumb at arm's length in front of your left eye and in front of the lamp.
- Slowly move your thumb toward your face until it is directly in front of your open eye.

Results The farther your thumb is from your eye, the smaller your thumb appears and the more of the lamp you see.

Why? Your thumb blocked the light moving from the lamp toward your eye. The closer your thumb is to your face, the more light it blocks. Because Mercury is very close to the Sun, it blocks only a small portion of the Sun's light, as did your thumb when held close to the lamp. The shadow made by Mercury is so small that it does not spread out enough to fall on the Earth, but lands in space. For this reason, Mercury does not cause a **solar eclipse** (blocking of some of the sunlight from parts of the Earth).

4. Thick

Purpose To determine why Venus' atmosphere is so hard to see through.

Materials flashlight
wax paper

Procedure
- Turn the flashlight on and place it on the edge of a table.
- Stand about 2 yards (2 m) from the table.
- Face the light and observe its brightness.
- Hold the sheet of wax paper in front of your face.
- Look through the wax paper at the light.

Results The light looks blurred through the paper.

Why? The light rays bend and bounce off the wax paper. This is similar to the way sunlight bends and bounces off the thick clouds that surround Venus, which are not particularly dark, just very thick. In their thickest part, the visibility is about 0.6 miles (1 km) or less. This low visibility would result in the closing of most airports on Earth.

5. Hot Box

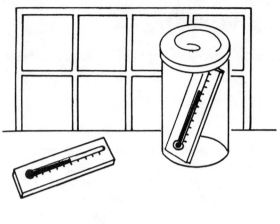

Purpose To determine why Venus is so hot.

Materials 2 thermometers
1 jar with lid (tall enough to hold one of the thermometers)

Procedure
■ Put one thermometer inside the jar and close the lid.
■ Place the second thermometer and the jar near a window in direct sunlight.
■ Record the temperature on both thermometers after 20 minutes.

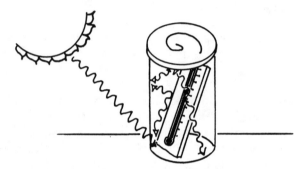

Results The temperature inside the closed jar is higher than outside the jar.

Why? The glass jar is used to simulate the trapping of infrared light waves by gasses in the atmosphere around planets. The thick atmosphere around Venus allows short wave radiation through, but blocks long wave radiation. The trapped long wave **infrared light** warms the planet's surface to about 800 degrees Fahrenheit (427°C).

6. Sun Prints

Purpose To determine what might cause Jupiter's colored clouds.

Materials scissors
cardboard
double-sided tape
photographic paper (This can be purchased at a photography store, or ask your local newspaper or high school photography club for a sheet of outdated photographic paper. Keep it out of the sunlight.)

Procedure
■ Cut a heart shape out of the cardboard.
■ In a semidarkened room, use the double-sided tape to stick the heart to the glossy side of the photographic paper.
■ Take the paper outside and allow the Sun to shine directly on the paper for 1 minute.
■ Return to the darkened room and take the paper heart off the photographic paper.

Results The photographic paper is unchanged under the cardboard. A light-colored, heart-shaped design is surrounded by a dark background.

Why? The photographic paper turns dark only where light hits it. This change is because the light activates the molecules on the glossy surface of the paper. Scientists think that the colors in Jupiter's atmosphere may come from chemicals in the clouds that change color because of lightning or that the Sun changes the colors as it did the special light-sensitive photographic paper.

7. Hot

Purpose To determine if conservation of energy applies to friction between molecules in a dense atmosphere.

Materials your hands

Procedure
- Place your palms together.
- Quickly rub your dry hands back and forth several times.

Results Your dry hands feel hot when rubbed together.

Why? Friction between your hands produces heat energy, as does the friction between any moving objects. **Friction** is a force that tends to stop objects sliding past each other. The closer and faster the objects in motion are, the greater is the heat. This would make one think that the dense **atmosphere** around planets such as Jupiter would cause an increase in the surface temperature. The winds around Jupiter blow in excess of 800 miles (1,280 km) per hour. The atmospheric gases are constantly being rubbed together, but the temperature on the planet does not increase continuously. The temperature on the planet Jupiter remains constant due to **conservation of energy** (heat gained by one substance is equal to the heat lost by some other substance).

8. Charged

Purpose To determine why lightning continually flashes on Jupiter.

Materials scissors
ruler
thin sheet of plastic (plastic report cover)
wool cloth (use any 100 percent wool coat, scarf, sweater, etc.)

Procedure
- Cut a plastic strip about 2 × 8 inches (5 × 20 cm).
- In a dark room, hold the end of the plastic strip. Wrap the wool cloth around the plastic, then quickly pull the plastic through the cloth.
- Repeat this 5 or 6 times.
- Observe the cloth as you pull the plastic through it.

Results A bluish light is seen in the folds of cloth that touch the plastic.

Why? **Electrons** are negative particles that spin around a positively charged **nucleus** of an atom. Some of these electrons are rubbed off the wool and onto the plastic strip. The wool becomes positively charged and the plastic negatively charged. When the electrons leap from the plastic back to the wool, an electric spark is created. Flashes of light are continually seen through the clouds that swirl around Jupiter. The molecules in the **atmosphere** are briskly rubbed together because of the winds that blow up to 800 miles (1,280 km) per hour. The rubbing of the molecules in the atmosphere, like the rubbing of the wool cloth on the plastic, can result in electric sparks.

9. See Through

Purpose To determine how Saturn can be seen through its rings.

Materials scissors
ruler
white poster board
glue

black marking pen
straight pen
pencil
adult helper

Procedure

- Cut 3 strips from the poster board that are each 1 × 6 inches (2.5 × 15 cm).
- Evenly space the strips so that their centers cross.
- Glue the centers of the strips together.
- Use the marking pen to make two marks across the ends of each strip. Start the first mark ½ inch (1 cm) from the end of the strip and make the second mark 1 inch (2.5 cm) from the end.
- Ask an adult to insert the pin through the center of the strips. Use the pin to enlarge the hole so that the paper blades easily spin. Then stick the end of the pin in a pencil eraser.
- Spin the paper blades.
- Observe the spinning blades.

Results Two black rings are seen, but you can see through the spinning blades.

Why? Your eyes blend the color on the paper strips as they spin, producing what appears to be solid rings. The rings around Saturn are made of chunks of ice and rock. Their movement makes them appear to be a continuous surface as does the movement of the black marks on the spinning paper.

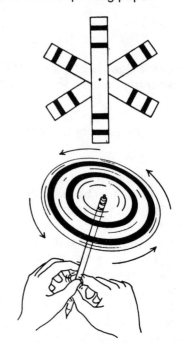

10. Spinner

Purpose To determine why planets move smoothly around the Sun.

Materials 10-inch (25-cm) diameter cake pan
pencil
sheet of paper
cardboard

scissors
ruler
heavy, thick string
4 large paper clips
adult helper

Procedure

- Use the cake pan to draw a circle on the paper and the cardboard.
- Cut the circles out.
- Fold the paper in half twice to find the center of the circle.
- Ask an adult to lay the paper over the cardboard circle and make a hole through the center of both circles with the point of a pencil.
- Discard the paper.
- Cut a 1-yard (1-m) length of string.
- Thread one end of the string through the hole in the cardboard circle, and tie a knot on the other side to keep it from pulling back through.
- Evenly space the 4 paper clips around the outer rim of the cardboard circle or disk.

- Hold the end of the string and swing the disk back and forth.
- Continue to hold the end of the string while you give the disk a quick spin toward you, then swing it as before.

Results The disk flops around when merely moved around on the string, but when spun, it rotates in the plane in which it was originally spun.

Why? The cardboard disk acts like a **gyroscope**, a kind of top whose axis always points in the same direction while spinning. The planets spin on their axis as they rotate around the Sun. This keeps them turning in the plane in which they were started just as the disk does.

11. On the Move

Purpose To determine why planets continue to move.

Materials round cake pan
pencil
1 sheet construction paper
scissors
1 marble

Procedure

- Use the cake pan to trace a circle on the paper.
- Cut the circle out.
- Place the pan on a flat surface.
- Lay the paper inside the pan and place the marble on top of the paper.
- Thump the marble so that it rolls around next to the wall of the pan.
- Remove the paper from the pan.
- Again, thump the marble so that it rolls around next to the wall of the pan.

Results The marble rolls in a circular path. It rolls farther and faster without the paper lining in the pan.

Why? **Inertia** is the resistance that all objects have to any change in motion. Inertia causes stationary objects to remain at rest and moving objects to continue to move in a straight line, unless some force acts on them. The marble stopped moving more quickly in the paper-lined pan because of **friction**. When the friction between the pan and the marble was reduced, the marble rolled for a longer time. The planets continue to move around the Sun because their movement through space is not restricted by friction.

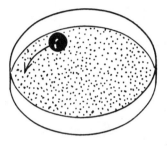

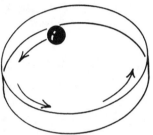

12. Speedy

Purpose To determine the effect of distance on the orbiting speed of planets.

Materials 1 metal washer
1-yard (1-m) piece of string

Procedure
NOTE: *This activity is to be performed in an open, outside area away from other people.*

- Tie the washer to the end of the 1-yard (1-m) length of string.
- Hold the end of the string and extend your arm outward.
- Swing your arm around so that the washer moves in a circular path beside your body.
- Spin the washer at the slowest speed necessary to keep the string taut.
- Hold the string in the center and spin the washer at the slowest speed necessary to keep the string taut.
- Hold the string about 10 inches (25 cm) from the washer and spin as before.

Results As the length of the string decreases, the washer must be spun around more times in order to keep the string taut.

Why? The washer seems to move sluggishly around in its circular path when attached to a long string, while on a shorter string, it zips around quickly. This is also true about planets, which differ in their distance from the Sun. As the planet's distance from the Sun increases, the pull toward the Sun, called **gravity** (the force that pulls celestial bodies toward each other), decreases. With less pull toward the Sun, the orbiting speed of the planet decreases. Mercury, the closest planet to the Sun, has the fastest orbiting speed and Pluto, the furthermost planet, has the slowest orbiting speed. (Twirling the washer on the string is not a true simulation of how planets move around the Sun, because planets are not attached to the Sun by a cord and do not move in a circular path.)

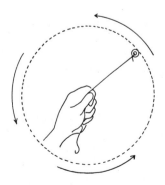

13. Expanding

Purpose To demonstrate how galaxies may be moving.

Materials 9-inch (23-cm) round balloon
black marking pen
mirror

Procedure
- Inflate the balloon so that it is about as large as an apple.
- Use the marking pen to randomly make about 20 dots on the balloon.
- Stand in front of a mirror and observe the dots as you inflate the balloon.

Results The dots move away from each other. Some seem to move farther than others, but no dots get closer together.

Why? Astronomers believe that the **galaxies** (large systems of stars) are moving away from each other similarly to the way the dots on the balloon move. Not all the galaxies are moving away from us at the same rate. In 1929, Dr. Edwin Hubble discovered that the farther away a galaxy is, the faster it seems to be

moving away from us. Since no two galaxies seem to be getting closer as they move, scientists believe the universe is expanding.

14. Balancing Point

Purpose To demonstrate the position of the Earth's barycenter.

Materials scissors
ruler
string
pencil
modeling clay

Procedure
- Cut the 12-inch (30-cm) length of string.
- Tie the string about 1 inch (3 cm) from the end of the pencil.
- Make a ball of clay, about the size of a lemon.
- Stick the clay ball on the end of the pencil with the string.
- Mold the clay around the string so that the string is barely inside the edge of the clay ball.
- Add a grape-size piece of clay to the opposite end of the pencil.
- Hold the end of the string and add small pieces of clay to the end of the pencil until the pencil balances horizontally.

Results The pencil hangs in a horizontal position.

Why? The **center of gravity** (balancing point) of the Earth-Moon system is called the **barycenter**. The barycenter is about 2,720 miles (4,352 km) beneath the Earth's surface on the side of Earth facing the Moon, and it is the point at which the Earth-Moon system moves around the Sun. The string represents the Earth's barycenter on the Earth-Moon model.

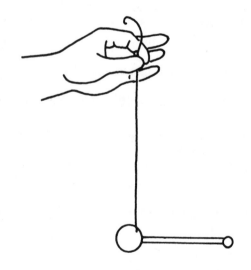

15. Lifter

Purpose To demonstrate how the atmosphere affects falling objects.

Materials paper
book larger than the paper

Procedure
- Position the paper on top of the book so that half of the paper is hanging over the edge of the book.
- Drop the book and paper from a waist-high position.
- Observe the paper and book as they fall and strike the ground.

Results The paper leaves the book and falls more slowly.

Why? Objects push against air molecules in the Earth's **atmosphere** as they fall. These air molecules push back against the falling object causing its speed to decrease. The speed of the falling book is greater than that of the paper because its **weight** (downward force due to gravity) is so much greater than the upward push of the air.

PAPER
BOOK

PHYSICS

16. In and Out

Purpose To demonstrate forces that keep satellites in orbit.

Materials scissors   masking tape
yardstick (meter stick)   thread spool
string   metal spoon

Procedure
- Cut 1 yard (1 m) of string.
- Tie one end of the string to the roll of tape.
- Thread the free end of the string through the hole in the spool.
- Tie the spoon to the free end of the string.
- Stand in an open area holding the tape in one hand and the spool with your other hand.
- Give the spool a quick circular motion to start it spinning in a horizontal circle above your head.
- Release the tape and allow it to hang freely.
- Keep the spoon spinning by moving the thread spool in a circular motion.
- Observe the movement of the tape roll.

Results The spoon spins in a circular path with only the weight of the tape pulling on the attached string.

Why? Any circling object, spoon or **satellite**, has a **centripetal force** (force directed toward the center) keeping it in its circular path. Moons that orbit planets and planets that orbit the Sun are all pulled toward the celestial body that they orbit. Their own forward speed keeps them from being pulled into the body that they orbit, and the centripetal force acting on the orbiting bodies keeps them from moving off into space.

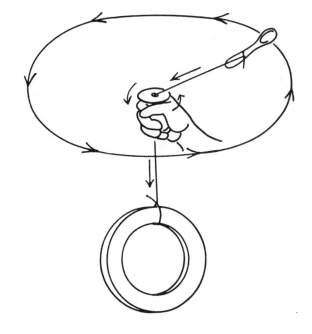

17. Same Place

Purpose   To determine why satellites appear to be stationary.

Materials   rope about 3 yards (3 m) long
helper

Procedure
- In an open area outside, use a tree or other object to represent the Earth.
- Ask your helper to hold one end of the rope as you hold on to the other end.
- Have your helper stand near the tree.
- Walk at a pace that keeps the rope tight and in a position so that you are in line with the same point on the tree as your helper.

Results   The person in the outside circle moves faster, but stays in line with the person moving in the smaller inside circle.

Why?   The distance around the outside of the circle is larger than the circle near the tree. A faster speed is required to travel around the larger circle in the same time that the person closer to the tree travels around the smaller circle. **Geostationary Operational Environmental Satellites (GOES)** are placed

at about 22,500 miles (36,000 km) above the Earth. They move at a very fast speed, which gives them an orbital period of 24 hours, the same as that of the Earth; thus, the satellites appear to remain stationary above the Earth. There are more than 120 geostationary satellites positioned above the Earth's equator.

18. Attractive

Purpose   To simulate the solar magnetic field.

Materials   bar magnet
8½ × 11 inch (22 × 28 cm) sheet of white paper
iron filings (found in magnetic drawing toys sold at toy stores)
small spray bottle
white vinegar
pencil

Procedure
- Lay the magnet on a wooden table.
- Cover the magnet with the sheet of paper.
- Sprinkle iron filings over the surface of the paper.
- Gently tap the paper with your finger until the filings settle into a pattern.
- Fill the spray bottle ½ full with the vinegar.
- Spray a fine mist of vinegar over the iron filings on the paper.
- Allow the paper to remain undisturbed for an hour.
- Lift the paper and shake the iron filings into the trash.
- Draw a circle in the center of the pattern left by the rusty filings and label it "Sun."

Results   The iron filings form curved lines around the magnet. Adding the vinegar makes the iron in the filings rust. When the filings are shaken off, the rust leaves marks on the paper where the filings were.

Why?   Every magnet has an invisible **magnetic field** around it. This field is made up of lines of force that attract magnetic material such as iron filings. The magnetic field of the Sun, like the bar magnet in this experiment, has a north and south pole. It is thought that the Sun's magnetic field may extend out of its north pole to the outer limits of our solar system (the orbit of Pluto) where it bends around and returns to the Sun's magnetic south pole.

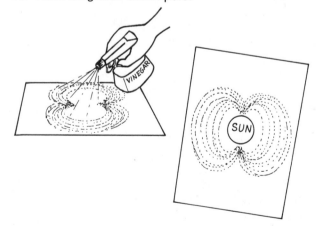

19. Free Movers

Purpose To determine why different parts of the Sun rotate at different rates.

Materials 2 2-quart (2-liter) plastic soda bottles
tap water
1 tea bag
washer (same diameter as the bottle's mouth)
paper towel
duct tape

Procedure
■ Fill one bottle ½ full with tap water.
■ Open the tea bag and pour the tea leaves into the water.
■ Cover the mouth of the bottle containing the water and tea leaves with the washer.
■ Turn the second bottle upside down and place it on top of the washer.
■ Use the paper towel to dry any moisture from the necks of the bottles.
■ Wrap strips of tape around the necks of the bottles to secure them together tightly.
■ Flip the bottles upside down and place the empty bottle on a table.

■ Support the lower bottle with one hand and place the other hand on the top bottle. Swirl the two bottles several times.

Results The water and tea leaves swirl in a funnel shape as they pour out of the top bottle. The leaves in the funnel move at different rates.

Why? As the water swirls, it pulls the leaves around with it. They are not connected so each piece moves according to the speed of the water at different parts of the water funnel. The Sun is not a solid body, but a ball of spinning gasses. Like the leaves, all the gases do not move at the same rate. Therefore, the number of days it takes for parts of the Sun to complete one **rotation** (turning of an object about its own axis) varies. The rotation time at the Sun's equator is about 25 days and about 35 days at its poles.

20. Radiate

Purpose To determine how energy from the Sun travels through space.

Materials baseball cap

Procedure
■ Stand outside in the direct sunlight.
■ Face the Sun for 5 seconds.
CAUTION: *Never look directly into the Sun because it can damage your eyes.*
■ Position the cap on your head so that it shades your face.
■ Stand with the cap on for 5 seconds.
■ Remove the cap, but remain in the same position for another 5 seconds.

Results The skin on your face feels warmer without the cap.

Why? **Radiation** is a process by which energy, such as heat, is transferred. Radiation also refers to the energy waves in the electromagnetic spectrum such as solar energy. The **electromagnetic spectrum** is a group of different energy waves that travel in a straight line at a speed of light which is 186,000 miles

(3,000,000 km) per second and do not require the presence of matter. Thus, solar energy can travel through space where there is no matter. Because the heat waves travel in straight lines, the brim of the cap was able to block the waves from your face. It took 8½ minutes for the energy waves to travel the 93 million miles (149 million km) from the Sun to your skin.

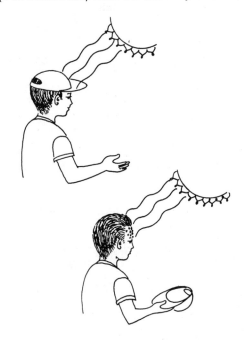

21. Blackout

Purpose To demonstrate a solar eclipse.

Materials coin

Procedure
- Close one eye and look at a distant tree with your open eye.
- Hold the coin at arm's length in front of your open eye.
- Bring the coin closer to your open eye until it is directly in front of the eye.

Results As the coin is brought nearer to your face, less of the tree is seen until finally the tree is no longer visible.

Why? The coin is smaller than the tree, just as the Moon is smaller than the Sun, but they both are able to block out light when they are close to the observer. When the Moon passes between the Sun and the Earth, it blocks out light just like the coin blocks your view of the tree. This is called a **solar eclipse**. The Moon moves around the Earth about once a month, but a solar eclipse does not occur monthly. The Moon does not orbit around the Earth's equator, and the

Earth's axis is tilted, so the Moon's shadow misses the surface of the Earth most of the time.

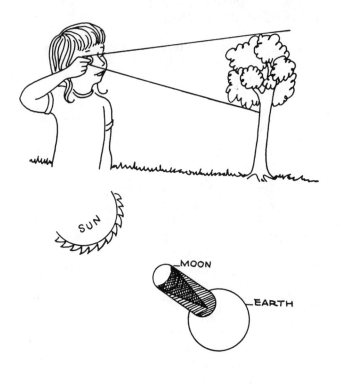

22. Swirls

Purpose To determine the color composition of sunlight.

Materials 1 sheet of white paper
clear, plastic ballpoint pen

Procedure
- Place the paper on a table near a window so that it receives the morning sunlight.
- Lay the pen on the paper so that the Sun's light hits it directly.
- Roll the pen back and forth on the paper very slowly.

Results Swirls of colors appear in the shadow made by the pen.

Why? The clear plastic acts like a **prism** (a transparent object that can break the white light of the Sun into its separate colors of red, orange, yellow, green, blue, indigo, and violet). You may not see each of these colors, but you can determine that there is a definite range of colors from red to violet.

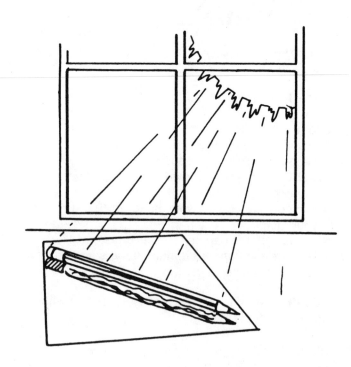

23. Clock Compass

Purpose To demonstrate how a clock can be used as a compass.

Materials scissors
ruler
1 sheet of white paper
pencil
12 × 12 inches (30 × 30 cm) cardboard
straight pin
clock
compass

Procedure
■ Cut a 6-inch (15-cm) diameter circle from the paper.
■ Write numbers on the paper circle as they appear on a clock.
■ Lay the paper circle in the center of the cardboard.
■ Stick a straight pin vertically through the center of the paper circle and into the cardboard.
■ Place the cardboard on an outside surface in direct sunlight.
■ Turn the paper circle until the shadow of the pin falls on the correct time. Do not use daylight savings time.

Results North will be halfway between the shadow and the number 12 on your paper clock.

NOTE: *Use a compass to check the accuracy of your clock compass.*

Why? This compass is most accurate March 21 and September 23 when the Sun rises in the east and sets in the west. On these dates, the shadow of the pin approaches due north as noon nears. At other times of the year, the clock compass loses accuracy, but the general direction of north can be found.

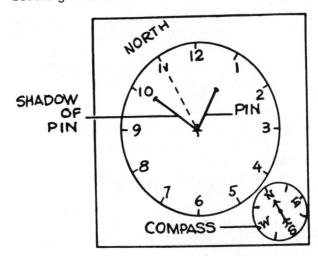

24. Mirage

Purpose To determine why the Sun's image is seen before sunrise and after sunset.

Materials modeling clay
small bowl that you can see through
coin
helper
pitcher of water

Procedure
■ Press a walnut-size clay ball into the center of the small bowl.
■ Stick the coin in the center of the clay.
■ Place the bowl near the edge of a table.
■ Stand near the table so that you can see the entire coin.
■ Slowly move backwards until the coin is just barely out of sight.
■ Ask your helper to fill the bowl with water.

Results The coin is visible and appears to be in a different position in the bowl.

Why? Light from the coin changes direction as it leaves the water and enters the air. This makes the coin appear to be in a different place. This change in the direction of light is called **refraction**. The Earth's **atmosphere** refracts light in a similar way, causing the image of the Sun to appear before the actual Sun rises above the horizon at sunrise and lingers after the Sun moves below the horizon at sunset.

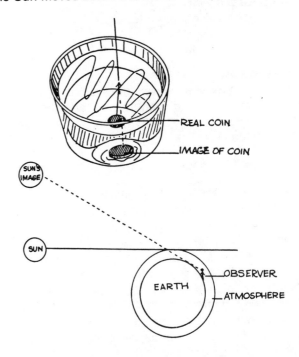

25. Slanted

Purpose To determine why the poles of Mars and the Earth are cold.

Materials 2 felt-tipped marking pens
1 sheet of white paper
compass
protractor

Procedure

- Draw a half circle on the paper with a diameter of 8 inches (20 cm) using the compass.
- Use the protractor to identify a 90-degree angle to the paper. Hold the two markers vertically so that they stand side by side.
- Press the markers against the paper to make dots.
- Lift both markers off the paper.
- Hold the markers on top of one another at about a 10-degree angle to the paper. (Use a protractor to measure the angle.)
- Lower the markers until the tip of the lower marker touches the paper within the top of the circle.
- Slide the top marker down until its point touches the paper and press to make a second dot on the paper.
- Compare the distance between the dots at the center to those at the top of the circle.

Results The dots made by the slanted markers are farther apart.

Why? The standing markers represent direct rays from the Sun and the leaning markers represent slanting solar rays. Just like the marks left by the pen, the distance between slanting solar rays is greater. Areas that receive direct rays from the Sun are much hotter. The Earth's equator receives about 2½ times as much heat during the year as does the area around the poles. Mars, like the Earth, has colder pole areas. Both of these planets are slightly tilted from the path of the Sun's rays, causing the center to receive more direct solar rays than do the poles.

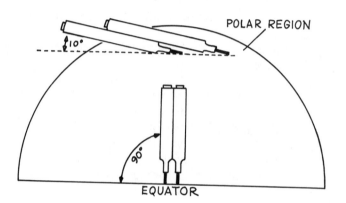

26. Distortion

Purpose To determine how the atmosphere affects the viewed shape of the Sun.

Materials pencil
1 sheet of white paper
compass
magnifying lens

Procedure

- In the center of the paper, draw a circle with about a 1-inch (2.5-cm) diameter using the compass.
- Look through the magnifying lens at the circle.
- Move the lens back and forth as you view the circle.

Results The shape of the circle becomes distorted.

Why? The glass in the magnifying lens has different thicknesses. As light passes through the lens, it changes directions. This change of the light's direction is called **refraction**. The thicker the lens, the more the light is refracted and the more distorted is the circle. The apparent flattening of the Sun at dusk, when it is near the horizon, is due to refraction of light. The rays from the bottom edge of the Sun are closer to the horizon and therefore travel through more of the Earth's **atmosphere** than the rays from the top edge of the Sun. These rays bend toward the Earth as they travel through the thicker section of the atmosphere. The atmosphere, like the magnifying lens, changes the direction of light passing through it, thus distorting the image seen.

CAUTION: *Be very careful never to look directly at the Sun when performing this experiment. Even the setting Sun can burn the delicate retina in your eyes.*

27. Sky Path

Purpose To demonstrate the apparent path of the Sun across the sky.

Materials pencil
sheet of white paper
2-quart (2-liter) round glass bowl
marking pen
compass

Procedure

- Mark an X in the center of the paper.
- Place the paper outside in direct sunlight.
- Turn the bowl upside down over the paper, having the X in the center of the bowl.
- Touch the sides of the bowl with the tip of the pencil so that the shadow of the pencil's tip falls on the X mark.
- With the pen, make a dot on the glass where the pencil touches the glass.
- Continue to make marks every hour throughout the day.
- Use a compass to determine the direction of the Sun's movement.

Results A curved path starting in the eastern sky and ending in the western sky is marked on the glass as the Sun appears to move across the sky.

Why? The Sun is not moving from east to west, but rather the Earth is turning toward the east. The Earth rotates once every 24 hours, giving the illusion that the Sun rises in the east, reaches its highest point in the sky at noon, and then begins to sink in the west. Because the Earth's axis is tilted, the Sun actually rises due east and sets due west only during spring and fall months. In the winter months, the Sun rises in the southeast and sets in the southwest. In the summer months, the Sun rises in the northeast and sets in the northwest.

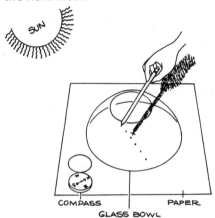

COMPASS   PAPER
GLASS BOWL

28. Blasters

Purpose To determine what might have produced the craters on the Moon.

Materials 2-quart (2-liter) plastic bowl
flour
3 or 4 sheets of newspaper
baseball

Procedure

- Fill the bowl ¾ full with flour.
- Spread the newspaper on the floor.
- Place the bowl of flour in the center of the newspaper.
- Stand with the bowl at your feet and the ball level with your chest.
- Drop the ball into the bowl.

Results The balls sinks into the flour and some flour dust flies upward from its surface.

Why? The surface of the Moon is pitted with **craters** (holes) ranging in size from tiny pits called craterlets to large basins many miles across called walled plains. Most craters were probably caused by high-speed **meteorites** (stony or metallic objects from space that reach the surface of a celestial body) crashing onto the Moon. The baseball represents a meteorite crashing into the surface of the Moon (the flour). Unlike the baseball, the high-speed meteorites explode on impact and scatter over a large area leaving only a large hole behind.

29. Changes

Purpose   To determine why the Moon appears and disappears.

Materials   pencil
styrofoam ball the size of an apple
lamp

Procedure
- Push the pencil into the styrofoam ball.
- Position the lamp near a doorway.
- Stand in a darkened room facing the lighted doorway.
- Hold the ball in front of you and slightly higher than your head.
- Slowly turn yourself around. Keep the ball in front of you as you turn.
- Observe the ball as you turn.

Results   The ball is dark when you face the door. Part of the ball lightens as you turn and it is fully illuminated when your back is to the door. The ball starts to darken as you turn toward the door.

Why?   The light from the doorway lights up one side of the ball at a time—the side facing the lamp. As you turn, more of the lighted side faces you. The Moon behaves like the ball. Moon light is a reflection of the Sun's light, and only one side of the Moon faces the Sun. The Moon has phases because as the Moon travels around the Earth, different parts of its bright side are seen.

30. Reflector

Purpose   To determine how the Moon shines.

Materials   modeling clay
hand mirror
flashlight

Procedure
NOTE: *Perform this experiment in a darkened room.*
- Use a piece of clay to hold the mirror upright on the table.
- Hold the front of the flashlight at an angle to the mirror.
- Turn the flashlight on then off.

Results   The mirror looks bright and a circle of light is seen on the wall.

Why?   The mirror does not give off light, but can reflect light. A beam of light reflects from the mirror and hits a wall when the flashlight is on. The Moon is not a **luminous body** (object that gives off its own light). The Moon only reflects light from the Sun. Without the Sun, there would be no moonlight.

31. Sender

Purpose To determine how starlight travels.

Materials rectangular baking dish
tap water
2 ping pong balls

Procedure
- Place the dish on a table.
- Fill the dish with about 1 inch (2.5 cm) of water.
- Place a ball on the surface of the water at each end of the dish.
- Push one of the balls beneath the surface of the water and release it.
- Observe the balls and any movement of the surface of the water.

Results The submerged ball rises and waves move quickly toward the second ball. The second ball rises and falls.

Why? Pushing the ball into the water causes the water to rise and fall in waves. Like a water wave, a wave of light from a star or any light source is a rising and falling disturbance that transfers energy from one point to another without the actual transfer of the ma-

terial. The energy of the moving water is transferred from one water molecule to the next, causing waves to move across the surface of the water and lifting the second ball.

32. Spreader

Purpose To demonstrate how distance affects a star's apparent brightness.

Materials flashlight

Procedure
NOTE: *Perform this experiment in a darkened room.*
- Stand in the center of a darkened room and shine the flashlight at a wall.
- Slowly walk toward the wall and observe how the light pattern produced on the wall changes.

Results The light pattern becomes brighter and smaller as the flashlight nears the wall.

Why? Light moves away from the flashlight in a straight line. If the beam of light leaves the light source at an angle, it continues to spread out until it hits an object. Other light sources, such as stars, behave in the same manner. Two stars giving off the same amount of light, but at different distances from the Earth, will appear to have different **magnitudes** (degrees of brightness). The spreading of the light from the most distant star results in less light hitting the Earth. Thus, the distant star appears dimmer, as

did the light when the flashlight was farthest from the wall.

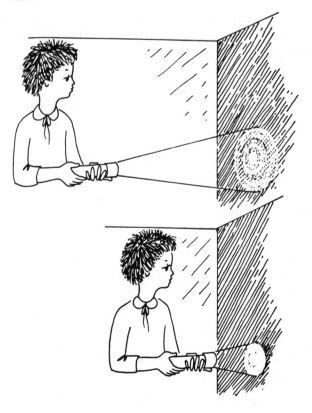

33. Hazy

Purpose To demonstrate why the Milky Way appears to be a hazy cloud.

Materials   paper hole punch
white paper
glue
black construction paper
masking tape

Procedure
- Use the hole punch to cut about 20 circles from the white paper.
- Glue the circles very close together, but not overlapping, in the center of the black paper.
- Tape the paper to a tree or any outside object.
- Stand close and look at the paper, then slowly back away until the separate circles can no longer be seen.

Results The separate circles can be seen when standing close to the paper, but at a distance, the circles blend together to form one large white shape.

Why? Due to the inability of our eye to distinguish discrete points of light that are too close together, the separate circles blend together as does the light from distant stars. Using binoculars or a telescope helps our eyes to see stars more clearly. The Milky Way **galaxy** is a group of stars including our Sun. That galaxy appears as a milky haze in the night sky. This hazy light is actually light from billions of stars so far away that their light blurs. This haziness is partly due to the inability of our eyes to separate distant light sources, but great amounts of galactic dust also scatter and block the starlight from the Milky Way.

34. Unequal

Purpose To determine why variable stars pulsate.

Materials   9-inch (23-cm) round balloon

Procedure
- Partially inflate the balloon. Keep the end of the balloon in your mouth during the experiment.
- Use the pressure of your breath to keep the air from escaping.
- Force more air into the balloon.
- Allow some of the air to escape.

Results The balloon increases and decreases in size.

Why? The balloon changes in size because the air pressure inside the balloon changes, and the balloon stretches and shrinks as the air inside changes. **Cepheids** (stars that have regular pulsations) are variable stars that, like the balloon, change size depending on internal pressures. These stars, unlike others, are not at equilibrium, meaning that their gravity pulling inward does not equal the pressure due to heat pushing outward. As cepheids change size, they also change temperature and give off a different amount of light. When hottest, the star appears yellow and when cool, it looks orange.

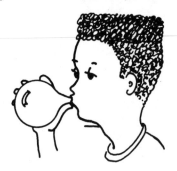

GRAVITY

35. Burn Out!

Purpose To determine the cause of "shooting stars."

Materials hammer
nail
block of wood

Procedure
- Partially hammer the nail into the wooden block.
- Carefully touch the head of the nail with your fingers.

Results The nail head is hot.

Why? Rubbing two objects together causes **friction**. Friction between the hammer and the nail produces heat as does the rubbing together of a **meteor** and air molecules in the Earth's **atmosphere**. **Meteoroids** are variable-sized pieces of materials floating through space. If the meteoroid gets close enough, Earth's gravity pulls it into the atmosphere. The friction of the fast-moving meteoroid against the air molecules causes the meteoroid to heat up and glow. This glowing mass is now called a meteor. Meteors usually burn up before reaching the Earth's surface. The flash of light as the glowing meteor burns is called a "shooting star." Showers of meteors occur each year around January 3, August 12, October 21, and December 14 because on these dates the Earth passes through the orbits of various comets. Matter in the comet's orbit is pulled into the Earth's atmosphere. If a meteor reaches the Earth's surface, it is called a **meteorite**. Most meteorites are as small as dust particles or sand grains, but larger pieces have struck the Earth.

36. Silhouette

Purpose To simulate an absorption nebula.

Materials table lamp
1 sheet of white paper
pencil

Procedure
NOTE: *Perform this experiment in a darkened room.*
- Turn the table lamp on.
- Hold the sheet of paper about 1 yard (1 m) in front of the lamp.
- Place the pencil about 2 inches (5 cm) from the paper on the side facing the lamp.
- Look at the paper facing you.

Results A silhouette of the pencil forms on the paper.

Why? A **nebula** is a vast cloud of dust and gas in space. There are three classes of nebulae—absorption nebulae that block light, emission nebulae that glow, and reflection nebulae that reflect light from other objects.

The silhouette of the pencil simulates an absorption nebula, which blocks the light coming from behind it and appears as a dark silhouette. The shapes of these clouds in the heavens are due to the concentration of the particles making up the nebula that blocks the light of distant stars.

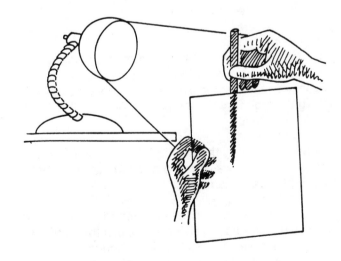

37. Star Chart

Purpose To record the position of the Big Dipper and Polaris.

Materials   scissors   white poster paper
             ruler   marker
             string   helper
             large nail

Procedure
- Cut a string 12 inches (30 cm) longer than your height.
- Tie one end of the string to a nail.
- On a clear, moonless night, lay a sheet of white poster paper on the ground.
- Stand on the edge of the paper and point to a star in the Big Dipper constellation while holding the free end of the string, allowing the nail to hang freely.
- Ask a helper to mark a spot on the paper under the hanging nail.
- Point to each of the stars in the Big Dipper as your helper marks their position on the paper.
- Find and mark the position of the North Star by drawing a straight line from the two pointer stars in the bowl of the Big Dipper to the star in the handle of the Little Dipper constellation.

Results The position of the **constellation** (group of stars that, viewed from the Earth, form the outline of an object or figure) called the Big Dipper is drawn on the paper and **Polaris**, the North Star, is plotted on the star chart.

Why? As your finger moves from one star to the next, the free hanging nail moves to a new position, thus plotting the position of the stars. Polaris, the star that the Earth's imaginary axis points to, is also called the North Star. This star can be found by following the two pointer stars, Dubhe and Merak, in the bowl of the Big Dipper.

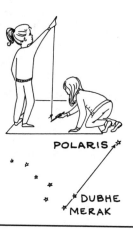

38. How Far?

Purpose To demonstrate why it would be useful to place a large optical telescope on the Moon.

Materials   clear plastic report folder
             freezer

Procedure
- Look through the plastic folder at a distant object.
- Place the plastic folder in a freezer.
- After 5 minutes, remove the folder from the freezer.
- Again, look through the plastic folder at the same distant object.

Results Cooling the plastic folder caused it to become cloudy. It was easy to see through the plastic before it was cooled.

Why? The moisture in the air **condensed** (changed from a gas to a liquid) on the surface of the cool plastic folder causing it to look cloudy. Clouds form in the Earth's **atmosphere** because of the condensing of water vapor similar to the cloudy covering on the plastic. There is no appreciable atmosphere on the Moon to form clouds so the view of distant objects is always unobstructed.

39. Details

Purpose To demonstrate the resolution of a lens.

Materials scissors
black construction paper
flashlight
masking tape
straight pen

Procedure
- Cut a circle of paper to fit over the end of the flashlight.
- Secure the paper to the flashlight end with tape.
- Use the pin to make two holes in the center of the paper circle about the width of the pencil lead apart.
- Place the flashlight on a table.
- Stand near the flashlight, facing the two spots of light emitted.
- Slowly walk backwards until the spots look like one dot.

Results The two holes appear as one beam of light from a distance.

Why? Resolution measures the ability to see details. This is true with your eyes as well as with telescopes. The resolving power of a telescope lens indicates the lens's ability to distinguish between the images of two points. The greater the resolution, the better one can see the object studied. The resolving power of a lens increases with the diameter of the lens. Atmospheric conditions also affect resolving power.

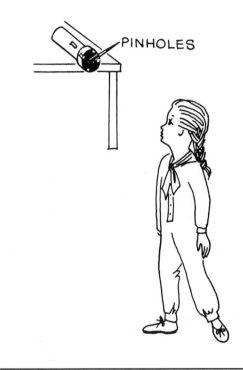

40. Streamers

Purpose To determine why a comet's tail points away from the Sun.

Materials modeling clay
scissors
ruler
string
pencil
fan

Procedure
- Form a clay ball the size of a lemon.
- Cut four 6-inch (15-cm) pieces string.
- Use the pencil point to push one end of each string into one side of the ball. Space the strings equally around the front of the ball.
- Stick the pencil point into the bottom of the ball.
- Hold the ball in front of a fan with the strings pointing away from the fan.

Results The strings fly out away from the fan.

Why? The wind pressure from the fan pushes the strings away. The strings simulate the tail of a **comet** (cloud of frozen gases, ice, dust, and rock orbiting the Sun). Solar radiation pressure and solar winds cause the comet's tail, which is made of gases and dust, to stream out away from the Sun.

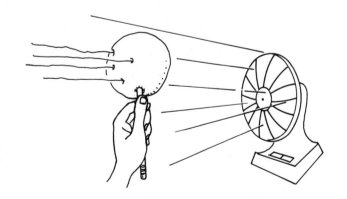

II
Biology

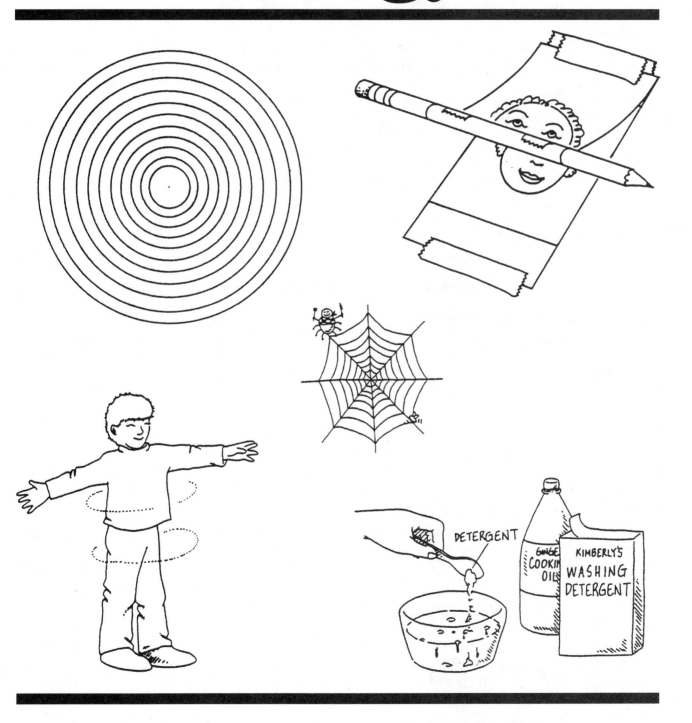

41. Water Flow

Purpose To demonstrate how water is transported through plant stems.

Materials   scissors
measuring cup (250 ml)
tap water
2 glasses
red and blue food coloring
1 white carnation with a long stem
(purchase at a floral shop)
adult helper

Procedure

- Have an adult helper cut the stem in half lengthwise from the end to about half way up toward the flower.
- Pour ½ cup of water into each glass.
- Add enough food coloring to make the water in each glass a deep color, one will be blue and the other red.
- Place one end of the flower stem in the blue water and the other end in the red water.
- Leave the flower standing in the water for 48 hours.

Results After 48 hours, the flower will have changed color. One side will be red and the other blue.

Why? Tiny tubes, called **xylem**, run up the stalk to the flower petals. The colored water moves through the xylem allowing the color to be distributed throughout the cells in the petals, causing their color to change. Minerals in the soil are carried to plant cells in this way providing nutrients to the flowers and leaves. The minerals **dissolve** in water (as did the red and blue coloring) and the solution is carried up through the xylem, from the plant's roots, to the leaves and flowers, and the rest of the plant.

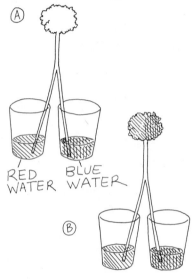

42. Hard to Freeze

Purpose To determine the effect of dissolved nutrients on the freezing rate of water. How does this affect the freezing rate of plants?

Materials   2 5-ounce (150 ml) paper cups
tap water
masking tape
marking pen
refrigerator
1 teaspoon (5 ml) salt
spoon

Procedure

- Fill both cups with water. Use the tape and marking pen to label one salt water and the other water.
- Add the salt to the cup labeled salt water and stir.
- Place both cups in the freezer.
- Observe the cups periodically for 24 hours.

Results The salt water never freezes as hard as the pure water.

Why? Salt lowers the freezing point of water. The pure water was able to freeze at a warmer temperature than the salty water. Plants freeze at different rates. Their surface area affects this, but it is also possible

that the amount of **dissolved** nutrients in the cell fluid affects their resistance to the cold. Farmers find that bean, cucumber, eggplant, and tomato plants cannot stand even the lightest frost while plants like broccoli, brussel sprouts, cabbage, and turnips can withstand heavy frosts. Some of these durable plants have large leaves. The materials dissolved in the leaves may help to make these plants more **frost** resistant.

43. Food Producers

Purpose To demonstrate that starch, a food substance, is produced in leaves.

Materials leaf, pale green
pint (500 ml) jar with a lid
1 cup (250 ml) rubbing alcohol
paper towels
shallow dish
tincture of iodine
adult helper

Procedure
CAUTION: *Keep alcohol away from your nose and mouth.*
- Place the pale green leaf in the jar. The paler the leaf, the easier it will be to extract the green pigment, chlorophyll.
- Pour the alcohol into the jar. Put the lid on the jar.
- Allow the jar to stand for 1 day.
- Remove the leaf and dry it by blotting with a paper towel.
- Lay the leaf in the shallow dish.
- Ask your helper to add enough iodine to cover the leaf.

CAUTION: *Keep iodine out of reach of small children. It is poisonous if swallowed. It stains clothes and skin.*

Results Dark areas appear on the leaf.

Why? Photosynthesis is an energy-producing reaction that occurs in the leaves of plants. Starch is indirectly one of the products of this reaction. Soaking the leaf in alcohol removes the waxy coating on the leaf and partially **dissolves** out the green pigment used in the photosynthesis reaction, **chlorophyll**. It is easier to see the results of the starch test without the presence of the green chlorophyll. Iodine combines with starch particles to form a dark purple to black color.

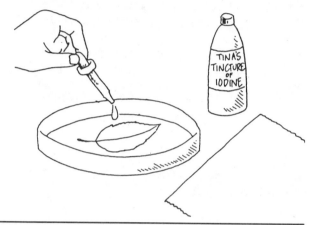

44. Desert Plants

Purpose To demonstrate the rate of evaporation from different leaf structures.

Materials 3 paper towels   waxed paper
tap water   2 paper clips
baking sheet

Procedure
- Dampen the paper towels with water. They should be wet, but not dripping.
- Lay one paper towel flat on the baking sheet.
- Roll up a second paper towel and place it next to the flat one on the pan.
- Roll the last paper towel as you did the second one, but cover the outside of the roll with waxed paper.
- Secure the ends, top and bottom, of the waxed paper roll with paper clips.
- Place the waxed paper roll on the pan.
- Position the pan with its paper rolls where it will receive direct sunlight.
- Unroll the paper rolls after 24 hours and feel the paper.

Results The flat towel is dry. The rolled towel is dry on the ends, but has damp spots inside. The waxed paper coated towel is damp all over.

Why? The more surface area that is exposed to the air, the faster the water evaporates. **Evaporation** is the changing of a liquid to a gas by increasing the heat content of the liquid. The speed that the water evaporates is called the **evaporation rate**. Desert plants have thick and/or round leaves to help prevent water loss. The surface of the leaves is waxy, further restricting water loss. The shape, thickness, and covering of desert plant leaves causes them to have a very slow rate of evaporation.

45. Baby Bean

Purpose To dissect a bean, identify the parts, and learn the function of each part.

Materials   10 to 12 pinto beans   tap water
                baby-food jar   paper towels

Procedure
- Inspect a dry bean and find the parts identified in the drawing.
- Place the beans in the jar and cover with water.
- To prevent souring, refrigerate the jar overnight.
- Remove the beans from the jar and place on a paper towel to absorb the excess water.
- Carefully remove the outer layer from one of the beans.
- On the rounded side, pry the bean open with your fingernail. Be very gentle as you open the bean.

Results What appears to be a baby plant is found inside the bean. If you do not find the baby plant or it was broken in the process of opening the bean, try again with another bean.

Why? The function of each bean part:
1. **seed coat**—protective covering
2. **cotyledon**—food for the growing baby plant
3. **micropyle**—small opening through which a pollen grain enters
4. **hilum**—where the bean was attached to the pod wall
5. **epicotyl**—forms the leaves
6. **hypocotyl**—forms the stem
7. **radicle**—forms the roots

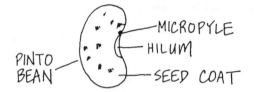

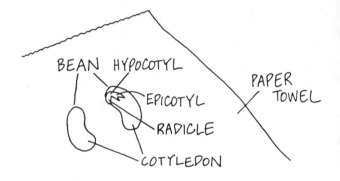

46. Lights Out

Purpose To determine the effect of sunlight on plant survival.

Materials   scissors
                black construction paper
                house plant
                cellophane tape

Procedure
- Cut two pieces of black construction paper large enough to cover one leaf on the plant.
- Sandwich the leaf between the two pieces of paper.
- Tape the paper together. It is important that the leaf not receive any sunlight.
- Wait 7 days.
- Uncover the leaf and observe its color.

Results The leaf is much paler than other leaves on the plant.

Why? A green chemical called **chlorophyll** gives leaves their green color. In the absence of sunlight, the green pigment is not produced, resulting in a light-colored leaf. Since chlorophyll is necessary for plant survival, the leaf will eventually die without sunlight.

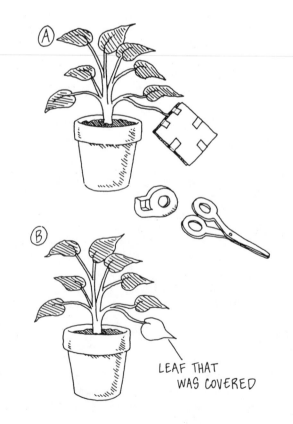

47. Cuttings

Purpose To grow a new plant from a cutting.

Materials house plant, such as ivy
scissors
small jar
tap water

Procedure
- Cut off a stem with leaves from the plant.
- Place the cut end of the stem in the jar filled with water.
- Observe the bottom of the stem for several days.

Results Tiny roots start to grow.

Why? Many house plants and especially ivy will easily form roots on cut stems. This is one way in which plants produce new plants other than by seed growth. For the plant top to continue to grow, it must be planted in soil or nutrients must be added to the water.

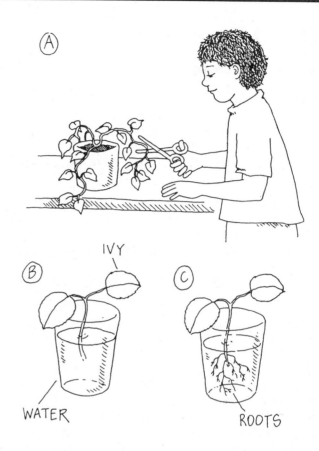

48. Eyes Up

Purpose To show that potatoes can propagate.

Materials 4 potatoes
quart (liter) jar
potting soil
tap water
adult helper

Procedure
- Place the potatoes inside a dark cabinet. Check the skin of each potato daily for small white growths called "eyes."
- Ask an adult helper to cut a square out of the potato around the eye.
- Fill the jar with potting soil.
- Bury the "eye" about 2 inches (5 cm) below the soil's surface with the eye sticking up.
- Keep the soil moist with tap water, but not wet.
- Observe the jar for 2 weeks.

Results In 10 to 14 days, a plant shoot will emerge from the soil.

Why? A potato is an underground stem called a **tuber**. The potato eyes are the organs of vegetative reproduction. Each eye will grow into a new potato plant. The production of a new plant from parts of an old plant is one way that potatoes **propagate** (reproduce).

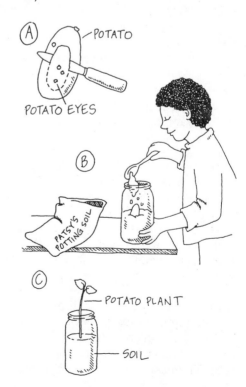

49. Algae Growth

Purpose To grow algae.

Materials pond water (collected by an adult from a lake, pond, or an aquarium that needs cleaning)
clear glass
pond plant (may be found at a pet store or lake)

Procedure
- Add the water to the glass.
- Place the plant in the water.
- Place the glass near a window that receives direct sunlight.
- Examine the glass after 7 days and then after 14 days.

Results The color of the water becomes increasingly green.

Why? There are 30,000 different kinds of algae. Many are green due to the abundance of the green pigment **chlorophyll**. Algae makes its own food, as do other plants, by a process called **photosynthesis**. The necessary requirements for this reaction are carbon dioxide, water, light, and chlorophyll. The algae grows in its sunny, watery environment producing more and more cells that contain the green chlorophyll. As the number of these cells increases, the water becomes greener in color.

Some algae are brown and some are red. It is the abundance of red algae that gives the water in the Red Sea its reddish color.

50. Compass Plant

Purpose To observe the water-absorbing ability of lichens. This explains the plants' north-seeking habit.

Materials compass
lichen samples (a pale green scaly or leaflike crust found on the bark of trees)
microscope or magnifying lens
eyedropper
tap water

Procedure
- Use the compass to determine the direction that the side of the tree with the most lichen growth is facing.
- Observe your lichen samples under a microscope or hand lens.
- Put drops of water on the lichen samples until they are wet.

Results Close observation of the lichen reveals that it has no roots, leaves, or flowers and is not one plant, but a combination of two. One plant consists of very tiny colorless strands and the other is round and green. The lichen absorbs water like a sponge.

Why? The strands of colorless cells are parts of a **fungus** (an organism that has both plant and animal characteristics). Since the fungus has no **chlorophyll**, it cannot make its own food, but it does act like a sponge and absorbs water and holds it. The strands also attach to the bark of the tree and anchor the plant. The green algae manufactures sugar and starch that it shares with the fungus. Lichen is generally found on the north side of a tree because moisture is a vital necessity for the plant and it survives best where it can retain moisture the longest. The north and northeast sides of trees have the most shade and thus a lower **evaporation rate**.

51. Coconut Cultures

Purpose To determine the best environment for mold growth.

Materials coconut   plastic bread sack
              rubber band   adult helpher

Procedure
- Ask an adult helper to break the coconut and pour out the liquid.
- Expose the open coconut to the air for 2 hours.
- Put the coconut pieces back together and secure them with a rubber band.
- Place the coconut in a bread sack in a warm dark place for 1 week.
- Look at the outside and inside of the coconut daily for any change, then discard the coconut.

Results The outside of the coconut seems unchanged while the inside develops different colored spots on it.

Why? **Mold** is a form of **fungus**, a Latin word meaning "food-robbing." The colored coconut garden contains different types of fungi that came from the air. They can not make their own food because they have no **chlorophyll** so they must steal food from their host organism. Fungi are all around you—in the air, on your clothes, skin, hair—everywhere. They must have air, food, and water to live. When they land on a nice moist airy piece of food like your coconut, they thrive very well.

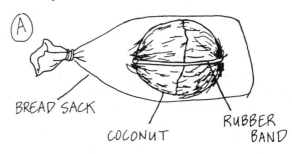

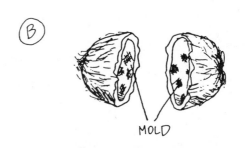

---

52. Dippers

Purpose To demonstrate how the internal compasses of some bacteria work.

Materials bar magnet (with North and South poles marked)
              sewing needle
              scissors
              ruler
              sewing thread

Procedure
- Lay the magnet on a wooden table.
- Place the needle on top of the magnet with its eye pointing toward the south pole of the magnet.
- Allow the needle to remain on top of the magnet for at least 2 minutes.
- Cut a 12-inch (30-cm) piece of thread, and tie it to the center of the needle. (Don't put the thread through the eye of the needle.)
- Hold the free end of the thread with one hand. Move the needle back and forth through the knot in the thread until it hangs in a horizontal position (level with the tabletop).
- Move your arm so that the needle is about 2 inches (5 cm) above the center of the magnet.
- Slowly move the hanging needle toward the north end of the magnet.

Results The sharp end of the needle points downward toward the north end of the magnet.

Why? Laying the needle on the magnet causes it to become magnetized. The magnetized needle lines up with the magnetic field around the magnet so the point of the needle is attracted to the north pole of the magnet. Some **bacteria** (microscopic organisms) have a chain of magnetic crystals called **magnetite** inside them and, like the magnetized needle in this experiment, they respond to **magnetic force fields**. Since the Earth has a magnetic force field around it, bacteria in the Northern Hemisphere with magnetite crystals are directed northward by their body compass. Not only does their body compass point north, but it also points a little downward which directs them toward the bottom of their watery homes.

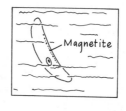

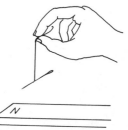

53. Flashers

Purpose To determine if you can communicate with fireflies.

Materials flashlight
fireflies, in a jar

Procedure

NOTE: *This experiment is done in a darkened room.*

- Hold the flashlight near the jar of fireflies.
- Turn the light on and off at 1 second intervals. (The easiest way to judge a 1-second interval is to say the words "One thousand and one.")
- Flash the light at least 10 times.
- Change the intervals to 2 seconds, then 3, and finally 4 seconds.
- Flash the light at least 10 times for each time interval.
- Observe the response of the fireflies.
- When you are done, release the fireflies outdoors.

Results The fireflies seem to respond to the light flashes.

Why? Fireflies are beetles that have a layer of light-producing cells on their abdomen. These cells contain **luciferin**, a chemical that gives off light when com-

bined with oxygen. The female has no wings and can be found on the ground. Her light is much brighter. It is believed that the rhythm of flashes attracts a mate. Fireflies usually flash their light in time intervals ranging from 1 to 4 seconds depending on the species. Different species have different response times.

FIREFLIES

FLASHLIGHT

54. Telegraph Lines

Purpose To determine how a spider evaluates the size of an intruder.

Materials string
helper

Procedure

- Stretch the string between two stationary objects. A door knob and a table leg are good choices.
- Gently place the tips of your fingers on top of one end of the string.
- Have your helper pluck the opposite end of the string while you look away.
- Your helper should pluck the strings with varying degrees of firmness: gently to very firm. You do not want to see how firmly the string is being plucked.

Results You will be able to feel the varying degrees of vibrations of the string with your finger tips.

Why? When the string is plucked at one end, it causes the entire string to vibrate. A gentle touch produces a weak **vibration** (back-and-forth movement of material) and a more aggressive plucking causes the entire string to vibrate briskly. Spiders

feel the vibration of their web. The web acts like a telegraph line. When the web shakes, the spider senses the movement because it has sensory hair on its legs. If the vibration is very weak, the spider ignores it. Very large vibrations could mean a prey that would injure the spider so it often hides or cuts the strand. A medium vibration lets the spider know that the intruder is small enough to catch for dinner and it rushes toward the source of vibration. The spider quickly wraps the trapped visitor in strands of silk before it can escape from the sticky web.

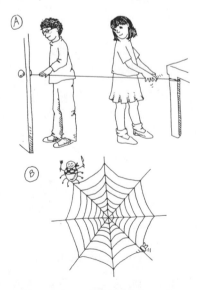

55. Flip-Flop

Purpose To determine how honeybees find their way home.

Materials
scissors
sheet of white paper
small bowl
marker
tap water
sponge
sewing needle
bar magnet
(with north
and south
poles marked)

Procedure
- Cut a paper ring to fit around the outside of the bowl.
- Use the marker to write the four compass directions N, E, S, and W on the paper ring.
- Fill the bowl with tap water.
- Cut a 1 × 1-inch (2.5 × 2.5-cm) piece from a sponge.
- Place the sponge on the water and lay a magnetized needle on top of it. (To temporarily magnetize the needle, lay it on a bar magnet for 2 minutes with the eye of the needle at the north end of the magnet.)
- Rotate the paper collar around the bowl so that the point of the needle points to the N.
- Remove the needle and place it on the magnet for 2 minutes with the eye of the needle at the south end of the magnet.

- Again, place the needle on the floating sponge.

Results At first the needle and the sponge swing around so that the point of the needle faces north. Reversing the direction in which the needle is magnetized causes the point of the needle to face south.

Why? Some scientists believe that a honeybee finds its way home because of **magnetite** crystals, which are attracted by a magnet, inside the insect's belly. These crystals, like the magnetized needle, may act like a compass that lines up with the Earth's magnetic field. If the crystals in a bee have their poles flip-flopped, as did the needle, the bee's built-in compass needle would point south instead of north. This bee would fly in the wrong direction.

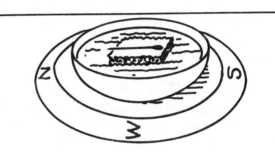

56. Belly Up

Purpose To determine why dead fish float, belly side up, on the surface of the water.

Materials
tap water
plastic sandwich bag that zips closed
drinking straw
large bowl

Procedure
- Pour the water into the plastic bag.
- Place the end of the straw into the bag.
- Zip the bag closed up to the straw.
- Fill the bag with air by blowing through the straw.
- Slip the straw out and quickly seal the bag.
- Fill the bowl with water.
- Place the closed bag into the bowl of water.

Results The bag floats on top of the water, air-filled side up.

Why? Fish have microscopic living things called **bacteria** (single-celled microscopic organisms) inside their intestines to decompose food. These organisms continue doing their job even after the fish is dead. When the food is **decomposed** (broken into simpler parts), gas is produced that balloons out the fish's intestines just as the plastic bag was inflated by your exhaled breath. Because the intestines of the fish are located on the underside, or belly, of the fish, the dead fish floats underside, or belly, up.

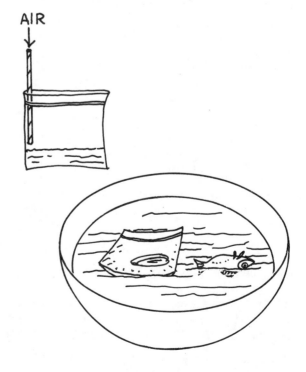

57. Blending

Purpose To observe that the color of animals protects them from predators.

Materials 4 wooden stakes
string
ruler
scissors
colored pipe cleaners (multiple colors)
timer
helper

Procedure

- Use the stakes and string to mark off a plot of grass about 20 feet (6 m) square.
- Cut 20 one-half inch (13 mm) pieces of each color of pipe cleaner.
- Ask a helper to scatter the pieces as evenly as possible in the marked off plot of grass.
- Pick up as many of the pieces as you can find in 5 minutes.

Results Some colors are easily found and others are more difficult. All of the pieces were not found.

Why? If the grass is the same shade of green as the colored pieces, it is difficult to distinguish between the two. Colors that look alike are harder to find.

Some of the darker colored pieces blend in with the shadows of the grass. A white bunny is hard to see when sitting on a field of snow, and green snakes blend in very well on a lawn of green grass. Thus, they are protected from their **predators** (animals that prey on other animals).

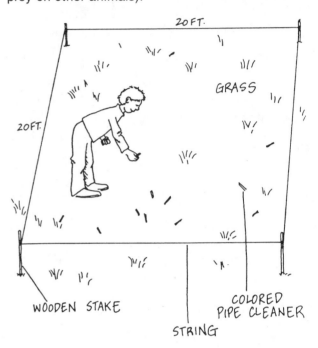

58. Ground Temperature

Purpose To determine why desert animals spend their day underground.

Materials trowel
2 outdoor thermometers
white towel

Procedure

- Dig a hole in an area with no grass. Make the hole 4 inches (10 cm) deep and large enough to insert one thermometer.
- Cover the hole containing the thermometer with the towel.
- Lay the second thermometer on top of the ground.
- Wait 5 minutes, then read the temperature on each thermometer. Be sure to read the underground thermometer as soon as it is removed from the hole.

Results The temperature in the hole is lower than that on top of the ground.

Why? The Sun's rays heat the air and all materials that they touch including the liquid in the thermometer. The soil on top of the ground gets much hotter because of the direct Sun's rays. The soil in the hole stays cooler because no direct heat is applied. Desert animals dig holes into the ground and stay there during the heat of the day to stay cool.

59. Foamy Nests

Purpose To simulate the formation of an African tree frog's nest.

Materials 1 raw egg
quart (liter) bowl
wire whisk
wooden spoon
adult helper

Procedure
- Ask an adult helper to separate the egg white and place it in the bowl.
- Beat the egg white into a thick white foam.
- Fill the spoon with a large mound of the white foam.
- Turn the spoon upside down.

Results The white foam hangs down from the wooden spoon.

Why? The hanging foam simulates the nest made by the African tree frog. The female frog prepares her nest by squirting out a slimy liquid. She whips the liquid into a foam with her back legs in much the same way as you whipped the liquid from the egg. The foamy nest is attached to a tree branch above water and eggs are laid into the foam. The squirming tadpoles that develop from the eggs break through the foam and fall into the water below.

60. Oily Feathers

Purpose To demonstrate the effect that polluting detergents can have on birds.

Materials 1 cup (250 ml) tap water
1 quart (liter) clear glass bowl
1 teaspoon (5 ml) vegetable oil
2 teaspoons (10 ml) powdered
dishwashing detergent
spoon

Procedure
- Pour the water into the bowl.
- Add the oil.
- Observe the surface of the water.
- Sprinkle the powdered dishwashing soap over the surface of the liquid.
- Gently stir the water to mix, but try not to produce bubbles.
- Again observe the surface of the water.

Results The oil spread out in large circles on the surface of the water before the addition of the dishwashing soap. When the soap was added, some of the oil sank and the rest broke up into tiny bubbles that covered the water's surface.

Why? Water is denser and does not mix with oil, thus the oil was able to float on the water's surface. One side of the soap molecule is attracted to water and the other side is attracted to oil. The large circles of oil no longer exist because soap allows the oil and water to mix. Soaps can cause a swimming bird to sink and drown. Birds stay afloat because of the oil on their feathers, which makes them waterproof. If the birds become soaked in water containing a high concentration of soap, the natural oil in the birds' feathers would break up into tiny droplets and allow water to penetrate the feathers. The bird would lose its waterproofing, the extra water on the feathers would increase the bird's weight, and it could sink.

61. Tangled

Purpose To determine one effect of plastic garbage pollution on sea animals.

Materials rubber band

Procedure
- Hook one end of the rubber band around your little finger.
- Stretch the rubber band across the back of your hand and hook the free end on your thumb.
- Try to remove the rubber band without touching anything.
- How is the garbage that is dumped in the ocean affecting the sea organisms?
- Seals and fish do not have hands. How can they remove the plastic rings from six-packs of beverages if they get these around their bodies?

Results It is very difficult to remove the rubber band from your hand.

Why? The plastic items in garbage are deadly to sea animals. Turtles swallow floating plastic bags because they mistake them for jellyfish. Their digestive tract becomes blocked and they die. Seals, fish, and other animals get plastic rings around their bodies and find them even more difficult to remove than you did the rubber band. These animals also often die. It may take as long as 300 years for plastic garbage to decompose in sea water.

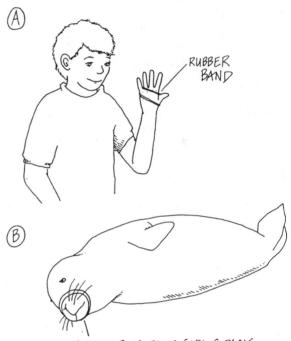

PLASTIC RING FROM SODA 6-PACK

62. Pollution

Purpose To observe the outreaching effect of a small amount of pollution on a stream and its wildlife.

Materials   measuring cup (250 ml)
tap water
1-gallon (4-liter) glass jar
red food coloring
spoon

Procedure
- Pour ½ cup of water into the jar.
- Add and stir in two drops of food coloring.
- Add 1 cup of water at a time to the jar until the red color disappears.

Results It takes about 7 cups of water to make the red color disappear.

Why? The red is visible at first because the molecules of red color are close together. As clean water is added, the color molecules spread evenly throughout the water. They finally get far enough apart to become invisible because of their small size. This is what happens with some water **pollutants** (substances harmful to living organisms). The material may be visible where it is initially dumped, but as it flows downstream and becomes mixed with more water, it is no longer seen with the naked eye. This does not mean that it is gone. Just like the red food coloring, it is still in the water and you would be ingesting small quantities if you drank the water. Similarly, animal life in stream is affected by pollutants many miles from the source.

63. Naked Egg

Purpose To demonstrate the semi-permeability of a cell membrane.

Materials 1 raw egg in its shell
1 jar with a lid (the whole egg must fit inside the jar)
clear vinegar

Procedure
- Place the egg inside the jar. *Do not* crack the shell.
- Cover the egg with vinegar.
- Put the lid on the jar.
- Observe immediately and then periodically for the next 72 hours.
- Keep the egg for Experiment 64.

Results Bubbles start forming on the surface of the egg's shell immediately and increase in number with time. After 72 hours, the shell will be gone. The egg remains intact because of the thin transparent membrane. The size of the egg has increased.

Why? The shell of the egg is made of calcium carbonate, commonly called limestone. When vinegar chemically reacts with limestone, it produces carbon dioxide gas—those bubbles seen on the egg. The membrane around the egg does not dissolve in vinegar, but becomes more rubbery. The increased size is due to **osmosis**, the movement of water through a cell membrane. Water always moves through a membrane in the direction where there are more dissolved materials, so the water in the vinegar moves through the thin membrane into the egg because the water inside the egg has more materials dissolved in it than does the vinegar. The contents of the egg stayed inside the membrane because these molecules were too large to pass through the tiny holes. This selectiveness of materials moving through the membrane is called **semi-permeability**.

BUBBLES of CO_2

VINEGAR

EGG WITH SHELL

DAVIN'S VINEGAR

64. Shrinking Egg

Purpose To demonstrate the semi-permeability of a cell membrane.

Materials corn syrup
ruler
jar with a lid (the egg must fit in the jar)
egg from Experiment 63

Procedure
- Pour corn syrup into the jar until it reaches a height of 3 inches (7½ cm).
- Carefully place the egg in the jar.
- Close the lid, and allow the jar to stand undisturbed for 72 hours.
- Compare the observation of the egg made in Experiment 63 with its appearance after soaking in the syrup.

Results The egg drastically changes in size and shape. It has a rubbery outer skin with very little content inside.

Why? The excess water inside the egg moves through the membrane into the syrup. The water content outside the egg is much less than inside, thus the water moves out of the egg. The molecules in the syrup and other materials inside the egg do not move through the membrane because they are too large. This selectiveness of materials moving through the membrane is called **semi-permeability**.

EGG

CORN SYRUP

KAY'S CORN SYRUP

65. Fooling Your Tongue

Purpose   To demonstrate how smell affects taste.

Materials   apple
eyedropper
vanilla extract
cotton ball

Procedure
- Take a bite of apple.
- Chew it thoroughly and swallow.
- Observe how the apple tastes.
- Add several drops of vanilla extract to the cotton ball.
- Hold the cotton ball near, but not touching, your nose as you take a second bite out of the apple.
- Continue to smell the cotton ball as you chew the bite of apple.

Results   Before you smell the vanilla, the apple has a regular apple taste. While smelling the vanilla, however, the apple seems to taste like vanilla.

Why?   The nerve endings on the tongue allow you to identify only four different basic tastes: sweet, sour, salty, and bitter. Other taste sensations are due to your sense of smell. The apple's smell influences how it seems to taste. When the apple's smell is masked by the strong smell of the vanilla extract, the apple tastes like what you smell: vanilla.

66. Trickery

Purpose   To demonstrate an optical illusion.

Materials   ruler
pencil
white paper

Procedure
- Use a ruler to draw two parallel lines 4 inches (10 cm) long on the paper. Draw the lines about 1 inch (1.25 cm) apart.
- Draw a V pointing inward at each end of one of the lines. See diagram A.
- At each end of the other line, draw a V pointing outward. See diagram B.
- Observe the lines and compare their lengths.

Results   Line A, with the V's pointing inward, appears to be longer even though we know that both lines are the same length.

Why?   This visual trickery is called an **optical illusion**. The direction of the Vs fool our brain into thinking that one line is longer than the other. Because your eyes follow the direction of the Vs, line A, with the ends of the V pointing out, makes the line appear longer than it really is.

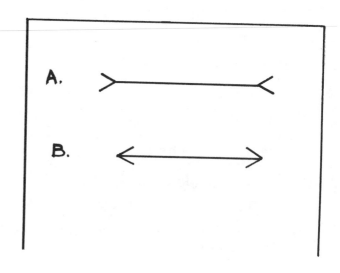

67. Wagon Wheel

Purpose To produce the illusion of a moving wagon wheel.

Materials diagram of circles

Procedure
- Hold this book with both hands.
- Quickly move the whole book in the smallest possible circular pattern with the center circle as the point of rotation.

Results The diagram appears to turn like a wagon wheel.

Why? The movement of the circles from one position to the next creates the illusion of motion. This is because of **persistence of vision**, which means the brain retains a visual image of the drawn circles after they have moved to another position. The retained image plus the real image make the circles appear to move.

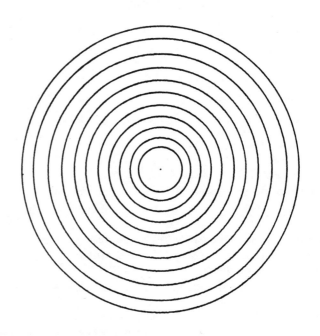

68. Blinking

Purpose To demonstrate persistence of vision.

Materials
scissors	pencil
ruler	cellophane tape
white paper	

Procedure
- Cut two strips of paper 2 × 4 inches (5 × 10 cm).
- Draw lines across one of the paper strips 1 inch (2.5 cm) from each end.
- Tape the top and bottom of this strip to a table.
- Between the lines and in the center of this strip, draw a face with one eye open and one eye closed.
- Lay the second paper strip on top of the first strip, with the edges of the strips lined up.
- Tape the top edge of this strip to the table.
- Trace the face on the top strip, but draw both eyes open.
- Tape a pencil to the bottom edge of the top strip and roll the pencil up to the line drawn on the strip as shown.
- Place your hands on the ends of the pencil.
- Roll the pencil back and forth quickly between the two lines on the strip several times.

Results The eye appears to open and close, as if winking.

Why? Rolling the paper strip back and forth allows you to see each face for only a fraction of a second. Your brain holds on to each image for about $1/16$ of a second. This retention of the image is called **persistence of vision**. When the next image appears in less than $1/16$ of a second, your brain doesn't register the transition. Because one of the eyes is in a different position in the two drawings, the overlapping of the images of the face gives you the illusion that the eye is blinking.

69. Vanishing Ball

Purpose To demonstrate the effect of the optic nerve on vision.

Materials   white paper
pencil
ruler

Procedure
- In the center of the paper, draw two, round ¼ inch (6 mm), colored dots, 4 inches (10 cm) apart.
- Hold the paper at arm's length from your face.
- Close your right eye and look at the dot on the right side with your open eye.
- Slowly move the paper toward your face. Be sure to concentrate on the right dot and *do not* look at the one on the left.
- Stop moving the paper when the left dot vanishes.

Results The left dot vanishes when the paper is about 1 foot (30 cm) away from your face.

Why? The light sensitive layer on the back of the eyeball is called the **retina**. Images are directed to this area by the eye's lens and the optic nerve carries the message of the image from the retina to the brain. The optic nerve enters the eyeball at the back and makes a break in the retina. If an image is projected to the spot where the optic nerve enters the retina the image is not seen because no message is sent to the brain. The spot where the optic nerve enters the eye is called the "Blind Spot."

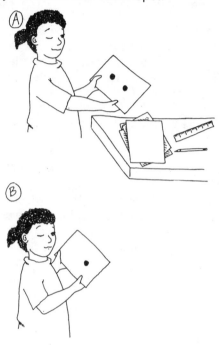

70. Water Drop Lens

Purpose A water drop is used to simulate an eye lens.

Materials   one 6-inch (15-cm) piece of 20-gauge wire
pencil
bowl
tap water
newspaper

Procedure
- Twist one end of the wire around the pencil to make a round loop.
- Fill the bowl with water.
- Dip the wire into the water with the open loop pointing up.
- Lift the loop carefully out of the water and hold it over the newspaper. You want a large rounded drop of water to stay in the hole of the wire loop.
- Look through the water drop at the letters on the page. You may have to move the loop up and down to find a position that makes the letters clear.

Results The letters are enlarged. If the letters look smaller dip the loop into the water again.

Why? The water drop is curved outward and acts like a **convex lens**. This type of lens is used as a magnifying lens and is the type of lens in eyes. Sometimes the water drop stretches so tightly between the wire that it curves downward forming a **concave lens**. This type of lens causes the letters to look small.

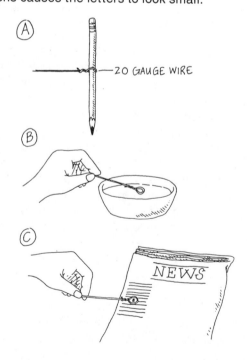

71. Night Vision

Purpose To demonstrate your ability to view contrasting colors at night.

Materials scissors
ruler
construction paper, black, dark brown, and white
cellophane tape
cardboard box about 1 × 1 × 2 feet (30 × 30 × 60 cm)
stool about 2½ feet (75 cm) tall

Procedure

- Cut two 4-inch (10-cm) letter V's wide from the brown paper and one from the white paper.
- Tape the brown letter at the top of the black paper and the white letter at the bottom of the paper.
- Tape the black sheet of paper in the bottom of the box.
- Place a stool in a dimly lit hallway or room.
- Place the box on the stool so that the black paper is upright and shaded by the shadow of the box.
- Stand so that you are as close to the box as possible, and are able to see the letters on the black paper.
- Observe how clearly each letter can be read as you slowly walk backwards about 15 feet (5 m).

Results The brown letter is harder to see at a distance than is the white letter.

Why? Contrasting colors are those colors that stand out against their background. The white letter has a high contrast against the black paper, and the brown letter has a low contrast with the black paper. In dim light or at night you have more difficulty viewing low contrasts, such as brown on black.

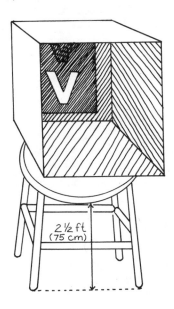

72. Sound and Direction

Purpose To test one's ability to determine the direction of a sound source.

Materials a helper

Procedure

- Have the helper sit in a chair.
- Tell the helper to close his or her eyes.
- Snap your fingers above his or her head and have the helper determine the area, front, top, or back of head that you snap your fingers. NOTE: *Be sure your fingers are held an equal distance between your helper's ears.*
- Do this several times changing the snapping position.

Results By random chance, some of the answers will be correct, but if enough trials are made, it will be obvious that the person cannot tell where the sound is coming from.

Why? The direction of sound is not always clear unless it is coming from a point directed toward the ear. If the sound is in the center of the head at the front, top, or back, one cannot tell the exact direction of the sound source. This confusion is due to the fact that in these areas the sound is received with equal intensity by both ears.

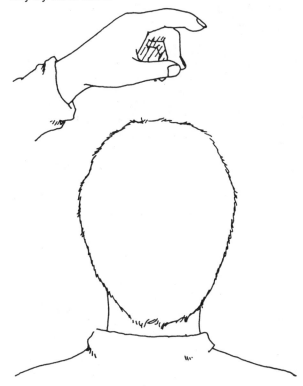

73. Change in Pitch

Purpose To make a model that demonstrates how human vocal cords change the pitch of sound.

Materials hammer
2 nails
ruler
wooden block about 8 inches (20 cm) long
short and long rubber bands
pencil
adult helper

Procedure

■ Ask the adult helper to hammer the nails into the board 6 inches (15 cm) apart.
■ Stretch a short rubber band between the two nails.
■ Pluck the rubber band with the pencil.
■ Replace the short rubber band with a long one.
■ Pluck the rubber band with the pencil as before.

Results The shorter band produces a higher pitched sound.

Why? The rubber bands behave similarly to the two folds of tissue stretched across the **larynx** or the

voicebox. These tissues are called the **vocal cords**. As air passes through the voicebox, the vocal cords vibrate. The pitch of the sound varies as the tension changes. When the cords relax, they vibrate slowly and the pitch is lower than when the cords are tightened.

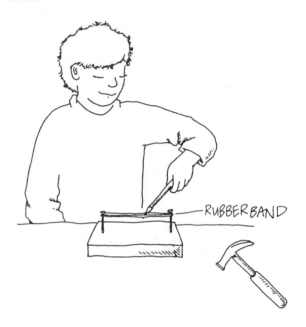

RUBBER BAND

74. Fingerprints

Purpose To collect and observe the patterns of finger prints.

Materials pencil
white paper
transparent tape
magnifying lens

Procedure

■ Rub the sharpened end of a pencil across a sheet of paper 15 to 20 times to collect a layer of graphite on the paper.
■ Rub your left index finger across the graphite on the paper.
■ Tear off about one inch (2½ cm) of tape and stick it across the darkened tip of your finger.
■ Remove the tape and stick it on a sheet of typing paper.
■ Repeat the process using the tips of other fingers.
■ Observe the patterns produced by each finger with a magnifying lens.

Results The patterns on each fingerprint are the same.

Why? The inner layer of skin called the **dermis** has projections. The outer skin layer, the **epidermis**, fits over these projections, thus taking on the same pattern. Each person has a fingerprint unique to that individual. These personal signatures form five months before birth and never change.

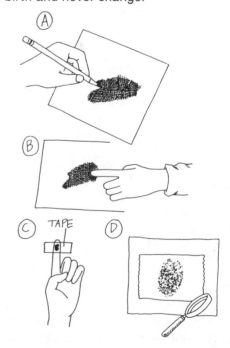

TAPE

75. Tendon Action

Purpose To determine how bones move.

Materials chicken foot (ask a butcher for this)
needle-nose pliers
adult helper

Procedure
CAUTION: *Wash your hands after touching raw chicken. It may contain harmful bacteria.*

- Ask an adult helper to cut away the skin around the end of the chicken foot to expose the white, string-like tendons.
- Use the pliers to pull the tendons one at a time.

Results The toes bend and extend.

Why? **Tendons** (strong bands of tissue that attach muscle to bone) are attached to both the outer and underside of the toe. When a tendon connected to the underside is pulled, the toe bends. Pulling a tendon on the outer side causes the toe to extend.

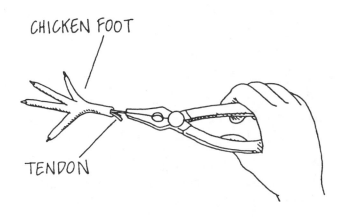

CHICKEN FOOT

TENDON

76. Lung Capacity

Purpose To measure the amount of air that can be forced out of the lungs.

Materials masking tape
1 gallon (4-liter) plastic milk jug with cap
tap water
plastic dishpan
2 feet (61 cm) of aquarium tubing
pen
helper

Procedure
- Place a strip of masking tape down the side of the milk jug from top to bottom.
- Fill the jug with water, and screw on the cap.
- Fill the dishpan about ½ full with water.
- Place the jug upside down in the water, and remove the cap.
- Have a helper hold the jug. DO NOT allow air bubbles to enter the milk jug.
- Place one end of the aquarium tubing inside the mouth of the jug.
- Take a normal breath and exhale through the tubing. Mark the water level on the tape.

- Refill the jug with water and return it to the dishpan.
- Breathe in deeply and try to exhale all of the air out of your lungs through the tubing. Mark the water level on the tape.

Results The water level drops as exhaled air enters the jug. Normal breathing does not push out as much water as does deep breathing.

Why? When the air enters the jug, it pushes the water out the opening. In normal breathing, only about one eighth of the lungs' capacity is used. During exercise, more air is taken in and exhaled, thus there is a larger amount of air exhaled during deep breathing.

AQUARIUM TUBING

77. Rubbed Off

Purpose To demonstrate how the epidermal cells are rubbed off.

Materials bar of soap
sheet of paper
course sandpaper

Procedure
■ Hold the bar of soap over the paper.
■ Gently rub the soap against the sandpaper.

Results The outer surface of the soap bar is rubbed off by the rough surface of the sandpaper.

Why? The outer layer of human skin, the **epidermis**, like the soap is constantly rubbed off, but unlike the soap human cells are replaced. We live in a world that constantly rubs, scrapes, grinds, cuts, and pushes against our skin. The outer layer is composed of dead cells that just fall off when touched. The body does not wear away as the soap did because there is a constant replacement of these lost cells by the under layer of cells. When cut, the cells grow back together. The epidermis is constantly changing and repairing itself.

78. How Do You Feel?

Purpose To test the sensitivity of different parts of the skin.

Materials two sharpened pencils
masking tape
helper

Procedure
■ Tape the pencils together so that the points are even.
■ Ask a helper to look away as you GENTLY touch his or her forearm with both pencil points. Be sure the points touch the skin at the same time.
■ Ask how many points are felt.
■ Do the experiment again, but touch the pencil points to the tip of the helper's thumb or finger.
■ Again, ask how many points are felt.

Results The helper feels only one point on the forearm, and two points are felt on the finger or thumb tip.

Why? The nerve endings in the arm and other parts of the body are too few to allow one to distinguish the separate pressures from the pencil points. The extra number of nerve endings in the finger and thumb tips allows one to make more accurate identifications. There is an increase in the pain experienced in areas with more nerve endings.

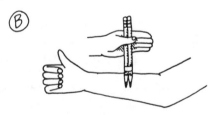

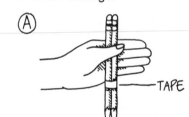

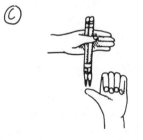

79. Spinning

Purpose To demonstrate the effects of spinning the body around rapidly.

Materials yourself

Procedure
- Stand outdoors in an open area.
- Turn around rapidly five times.
- Sit on the ground.

Results You will feel dizzy for a short time after you have stopped turning.

Why? The liquid in the canals of your ears begins to move as the body turns. When the body stops revolving, the liquid continues to turn, and this motion is interpreted by the brain to mean the body is still turning. Hence, you feel dizzy.

80. Change of Pattern

Purpose To test your power of concentration.

Materials a helper

Procedure
- Ask your helper to pat the top of his or her head with one hand and to pat his or her stomach with the other hand.
- Have him or her to continue patting the head, but to start rubbing the stomach in a circular motion.
- Reverse the movements and have your helper rub his or her head while patting his stomach.

Results It is easy for the hands to perform the same pattern of movement, but much concentration is necessary to successfully move the hands simultaneously in two different patterns.

Why? Through repetition of motion, you become proficient at moving the hands in the same pattern. Your brain is programmed to do this. Back-and-forth motions or circular motions are easily done, but only one pattern at a time. Both types of motion are in the brain's many programs, but it takes much concentration to activate the two programs at the same time.

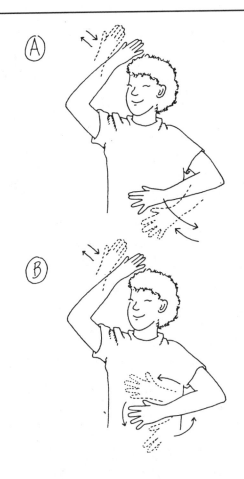

III
Chemistry

81. What's Inside?

Purpose To identify an unseen object.

Materials   ball of clay
a small object
toothpick
helper

Procedure

- Have someone secretly wrap the clay around a small object and mold the clay into a ball. The object must be firm enough so that the toothpick does not break it.
- Poke the toothpick into the clay ball about 15 times. Do not change the shape of the ball.
- Determine the size and shape of the object inside the clay.
- Guess what is inside the clay ball.

Results The size and shape can be determined and, if it is a familiar object, it will be identified.

Why? The depth that the toothpick is inserted into the clay gives clues to the size and shape of the object. The firmness of the unseen object is determined when the toothpick touches it. Scientists often make decisions about the size and shape of objects without seeing them. You are using a scientific method called **deductive reasoning** to identify the unseen object.

82. An Empty Sack?

Purpose To demonstrate that air is an example of matter and that it takes up space.

Materials   empty plastic bread sack

Procedure

- Fill the empty sack by opening the top and moving the sack through the air.
- Close the top by twisting the opening and holding it with your hand.
- Squeeze the sack with your other hand.

Results The sack resists being squeezed.

Why? The air molecules fill the sack and apply pressure to the inside. These molecules are pushing out more than you are pushing in. If enough pressure could be applied, the molecules would move closer together and the sack would deflate. You will not be able to apply enough pressure for this to happen.

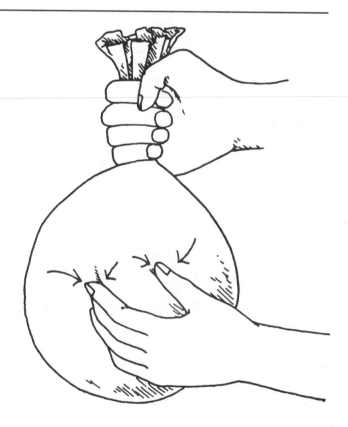

83. Not at the Same Time

Purpose To observe that two pieces of matter cannot occupy the same space at the same time.

Materials 9-ounce (270-ml) clear, plastic glass
tap water
masking tape
6 marbles

Procedure
■ Fill ½ of the glass with water.
■ Use a piece of tape to mark the top of the water level.
■ Very carefully add the marbles to the water by tilting the glass and allowing one marble at a time to slide down the inside to the bottom.
■ Set the glass upright and notice the water level.

Results The water level is higher with the marbles in the glass.

Why? Water and marbles are both examples of **matter**. Two pieces of **matter** cannot occupy the same space at the same time. When the marbles are

dropped into the jar, the water is pushed out of the way by the marbles. The rise in the water level is equal to the volume of the marbles.

84. Dry Paper

Purpose To demonstrate that even though gases cannot always be seen, they do take up space.

Materials bucket (taller than the glass)
tap water
1 paper towel
9-ounce (270-ml) clear, plastic glass

Procedure
■ Fill the bucket ½ full with water.
■ Wad the paper towel into a ball and push it to the bottom of the glass.
■ Turn the glass upside down. The paper wad must remain against the bottom of the glass. Make the paper ball a little bigger if it falls.
■ Important: Hold the glass vertically with its mouth pointing down. Push the glass straight down into the bucket filled ½ full of water.
■ Important: DO NOT TILT the glass as you lift it out of the water.
■ Remove the paper and examine it.

Results The paper is dry.

Why? The glass is filled with paper and air. The air prevents the water from entering the glass, thus keeping the paper dry.

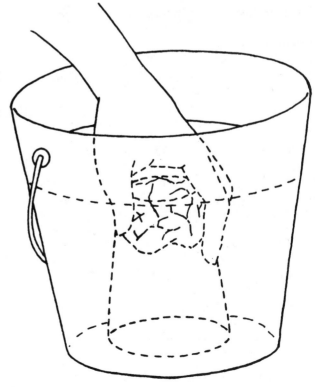

85. How Much?

Purpose To demonstrate that 1 + 1 does not always equal 2.

Materials   masking tape
clear, glass quart (liter) jar
measuring cup (250 ml)
tap water
pencil or pen
1 cup (250 ml) sugar

Procedure

■ Place a strip of masking tape down the outside of the jar.
■ Pour 1 cup (250 ml) of water into the jar.
■ Mark the water level on the tape with a 1 to indicate the volume occupied by 1 cup.
■ Add a second cup of water to the jar and mark the water level on the tape again. This time use a 2.
■ Empty and dry the measuring jar.
■ Pour the sugar into the jar. Make sure that the top of the sugar is at the 1-cup (250-ml) mark on the tape.
■ Add 1 cup (250 ml) of water and stir.
■ Observe the height of the liquid in the jar.
■ Keep the measuring jar for other experiments.

Results The liquid level is below the 2 on the tape.

Why? Water and sugar are examples of **matter** and therefore cannot occupy the same space at the same time. The cup of sugar is not solid throughout. Although you have put 2 cups (250 ml) of matter in the jar, there are spaces between the sugar grains. The water moves down into these spaces, resulting in a volume that is less than 2 cups (500 ml).

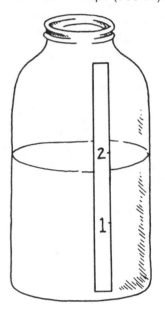

86. Where Did It Go?

Purpose To illustrate that there are pockets of space between water molecules.

Materials   blue food coloring
1 cup (250 ml) tap water
measuring jar (see Experiment 85 for instructions)
1 cup (250 ml) rubbing alcohol

Procedure

■ Add 5 or 6 drops of food coloring to the water to make the water level easier to see.
■ Pour the colored water into the measuring jar.
■ Add the rubbing alcohol to the colored water.
CAUTION: *Keep alcohol away from your nose and mouth.*
■ Observe the height of the liquid.

Results The liquid level is below the 2 mark.

Why? The connection of water molecules forms small empty pockets (see the diagram). These pockets are filled with the alcohol, causing the combined volume to be less than two cups.

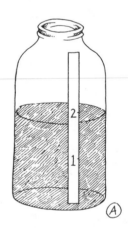

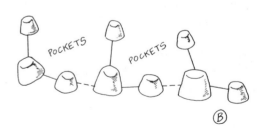

87. Sinker

Purpose To sink and raise an eyedropper by changing its density.

Materials 2-liter plastic soda bottle with lid
glass eyedropper

Procedure
- Fill the soda bottle to overflowing with water.
- Partially fill the eyedropper with water and place it in the bottle. The eyedropper should float, if it sinks, squeeze some of the water out of the bulb.
- Close the lid.
- Squeeze the sides of the bottle with your hands.
- Observe the level of water inside the eyedropper.

Results Squeezing causes the eyedropper to sink. When the bottle is released, the eyedropper rises.

Why? Squeezing the bottle increases the pressure inside, causing water to move into the eyedropper. This extra water makes the dropper heavier and it sinks. Releasing the pressure on the bottle decreases the pressure in the bottle and the excess water moves out of the dropper and, being lighter, it now rises. The eyedropper changes only its **weight** by the addition and loss of the water. Since its size remains constant, one can say that the density of the dropper changed. **Density** is a scientific way of describing "heaviness" of an object.

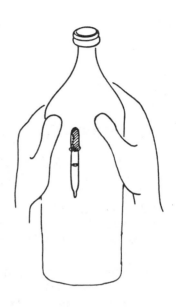

88. Tug of War

Purpose To demonstrate the difference in the pulling power of water and alcohol.

Materials ½ cup (125 ml) tap water
1 7-ounce (210-ml) paper cup
food coloring (red or blue)
1-foot (30 cm) sheet of aluminum foil
eyedropper
rubbing alcohol

Procedure
- Pour the water in the cup and add enough food coloring to make a dark solution.
- Smooth the sheet of aluminum foil on a table.
- Pour a very thin layer of the colored water onto the foil.
NOTE: *The thinner the layer, the better.*
- Add a drop of alcohol to the center of the thin layer of colored water.
CAUTION: *Keep alcohol away from your nose and mouth.*

Results The water rushes away from the alcohol leaving a very thin layer of alcohol on the foil. As the water pulls away, there is a pulsation around the edge of the alcohol.

Why? The water molecules on the surface of the water pull equally on each other before the alcohol is added. When the drop of alcohol touches the water, the two liquids separate immediately. Alcohol is pulling away from the water and the water is pulling away from the alcohol. The water molecules seem to be victorious and the water spreads outward taking some of the alcohol with it. This outward movement causes the alcohol to be spread into a thin layer over the foil. It also causes the water molecules to stack up and form a ridge around the alcohol layer. This ridge has a pulsating motion because the water and alcohol molecules continue to pull on each other. The pulling stops when the two liquids totally mix together.

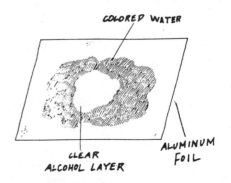

COLORED WATER

CLEAR ALCOHOL LAYER

ALUMINUM FOIL

89. Over the Rim

Purpose To observe that water can rise above the edge of its container, without spilling.

Materials cup and saucer
tap water
paper clips

PAPER CLIPS

Procedure
- Place the cup on the saucer.
- Fill the cup to the brim with water.
- Drop one paper clip at a time into the cup until the water spills over the rim. NOTE: *After the addition of each paper clip, look at the water's surface from the side.*

Results The water rises above the rim of the cup. The height of the water continues to rise as the paper clips are added. The water finally spills over the rim.

Why? Water molecules across the surface are attracted to each other. This attraction is strong enough to allow the water to rise above the top of the cup without spilling. The bulge of water above the rim finally gets so high that the molecules of water can no longer hold together, and over the rim they go.

90. Attractive Streams

Purpose To observe how separate streams of water form one stream when pinched together.

Materials 1 styrofoam or paper cup (no less than 6 ounces (180 ml))
pencil
tap water

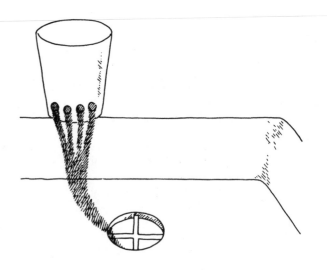

Procedure
- Punch four holes in the cup with the pencil. The holes are to be as close together as possible in a straight line at the base of the cup.
- Stand the cup on the side of a sink with the holes on the sink side.
- Fill the cup with water.
- Take your thumb and forefinger and pinch the four streams of water together.

Results Water pours out of the four separate holes. Pinching the streams causes the streams to unite. If the holes are close enough, one stream forms. If not, two or three streams will be formed.

Why? One water molecule has an attraction for another water molecule. These molecules will actually pull on each other and stick together.

91. Magic Solution

Purpose To float an egg in a "magic" solution.

Materials 2 clear, plastic cups
tap water
¼ teaspoon (1.3 ml) milk
3 tablespoons table salt
spoon
2 small eggs

Procedure
- Fill both cups ¾ full with water.
- Add the milk to one cup of water.
- Add and stir in the salt to the second cup of water. This will be referred to as the "magic" solution.
- Place an egg in each cup.

Results The egg floats in the "magic" solution, but sinks in the milky solution.

NOTE: *If the egg does not float in the magic solution, add more salt to the water.*

Why? The milk was added only to give the water a cloudy appearance like the "magic" salt water. The egg floats because it is not as dense as the salty water. The dense salt water is able to hold the egg up.

The egg in the milky water is denser than the water; thus it sinks.

92. Spheres of Oil

Purpose To demonstrate that gravity has little effect on drops of oil submerged in a liquid.

Materials ½ cup (125 ml) tap water
clear drinking glass
½ cup (125 ml) rubbing alcohol
eyedropper
cooking oil

Procedure
- Pour the water into the glass.
- Tilt the glass and very slowly pour in the alcohol. Be careful not to shake the glass because the alcohol and water will mix.
CAUTION: *Do not get alcohol near your nose or mouth.*
- Fill the eyedropper with the cooking oil.
- Place the tip of the dropper below the surface of the top alcohol layer and squeeze out several drops of oil.

Results The alcohol forms a layer on top of the water. The drops of oil form nearly perfect spheres that float in the center below the alcohol and on top of the water.

Why? The downward pull of **gravity** has little effect on the drops of oil because they are surrounded by liquid molecules that are pulling on them in all directions. The oil drops are also pulling on each other, and without the effects of gravity, the oil pulls itself into a shape that takes up the least surface area, a sphere.

93. Bubbler

Purpose To demonstrate the effect of gas pressure in a closed container.

Materials scissors
ruler
drinking straw
eyedropper
dishwashing liquid
saucer
½ cup (125 ml) tap water
½ cup (125 ml) white vinegar
modeling clay
1 teaspoon (5 ml) baking soda
bathroom tissue
glass soda bottle

Procedure

- Cut a 4-inch (10-cm) piece from the straw and wrap a walnut-size piece of clay around its center. Save the remaining piece of the straw to use as a stirrer.
- Place 2 drops of dishwashing liquid and 2 drops of water into the saucer. Stir.
- Pour the water and the vinegar into the bottle.
- Spread the baking soda across the center of the tissue section.
- Roll the tissue up and twist the ends of the paper.

- Drop the packet into the bottle. Immediately place one end of the straw in the bottle and seal the mouth of the bottle with the clay.
- Dip your finger into the soap and water mixture and rub the mixture across the open end of the straw.

Results A soap bubble forms at the top of the straw.

Why? The wet tissue tears and the baking soda and vinegar mix, forming carbon dioxide gas. The gas fills the bottle and goes up the straw. The pressure of the gas pushes against the thin soap film across the straw's opening stretching it outward to form a bubble.

94. Risers

Purpose To demonstrate why bubbles form in a glass of soda.

Materials scissors   plastic drinking glass
ruler   paper clip
paper towel   colorless soda

Procedure

- Cut a strip of paper towel 1 inch (1.25 cm) wide and about 2 inches (5 cm) longer than the height of the glass.
- Attach the paper clip to one end of the paper strip.
- Fill the glass with soda.
- Observe the contents of the glass.
- Lower the weighted paper-clipped end of the paper strip into the glass of soda.
- Observe the surface and area around the hanging paper.

Results Bubbles are seen throughout the glass of soda, but more form on the sides of the glass and on the surface of the paper.

Why? The soda contains tiny invisible bubbles of dissolved carbon dioxide gas. Any microscopic cracks in the glass or particles in the soda provide a place for the tiny bubbles of gas to stick, combine with other bubbles, and grow larger. The rough surface of the paper provides many places for the dissolved gas to stick. When the bubbles are large enough, they break away from the paper and float to the surface. Thus, a stream of bubbles rises from the surface of the paper.

95. Pop Cork

Purpose To shoot a cork from a soda bottle.

Materials ½ package dry yeast
soda bottle
warm tap water
1 teaspoon (5 ml) sugar
cork that fits the soda bottle
petroleum jelly

Procedure

- Pour the yeast into the soda bottle.
- Fill the bottle ½ full with warm water.
- Add the sugar.
- Place your thumb over the bottle's mouth and shake the bottle vigorously to mix the contents.
- Cover the sides of the cork with petroleum jelly.
- Loosely stopper the bottle with the cork.
CAUTION: *Do not seal the bottle with a cap or tight-fitting cork.*
- Place the bottle on the ground.
- Stand at least 6 feet (2 m) from the bottle.

Results After a few minutes the cork pops out of the bottle and into the air.

Why? Yeast is a **fungus** that uses sugar and oxygen to produce energy. As this energy is produced carbon dioxide is also formed. As the amount of carbon dioxide gas increases inside the closed bottle, the pressure of the gas builds. When enough gas is formed, the cork will be pushed out with enough force to produce a popping noise.

96. Drinkable Iron

Purpose To test for the presence of iron in fruit juices.

Materials 1-pint (500 ml) glass jar
3 tea bags
warm tap water
4 tablespoons (60 ml) pineapple juice
4 tablespoons (60 ml) apple juice
4 tablespoons (60 ml) white grape juice
4 tablespoons (60 ml) cranberry juice
5 clear plastic glasses
measuring spoons

Procedure

- Make a strong tea solution by placing the tea bags in the pint jar; then filling it with warm water.
- Allow the jar to stand for 1 hour.
- Pour each juice sample into a different glass, as shown in the illustration.
- Add 4 tablespoons (60 ml) of tea to each glass and stir. Wash the spoon with water after each use.
- Allow the glasses to sit undisturbed for 20 minutes.
- Carefully lift each glass and look up through the bottom of the glass. Make note of the juice that has dark particles settling on the bottom of the glass.
- Allow the glasses to sit for 2 hours more.
- Again, look for dark particles on the bottom of the glasses.

Results Dark particles are seen in the pineapple juice after 20 minutes. Particles are seen in the cranberry and white grape after 2 hours. No particles form in the apple juice.

Why? A chemical change takes place that is evident by the solid particles that form. The particles are not the color of the juices—another indication that something new has been produced. Iron in the juices combines with chemicals in the tea to form the dark particles. More particles formed in a faster time in the pineapple juice because it contains more iron. The quantity and speed of the formation of the dark particles indicates the quantity of the iron in the juice.

97. Sticky Sand

Purpose To discover how a non-Newtonian fluid behaves.

Materials   measuring spoons
tap water
2-quart (liter) bowl
1 cup (250 ml) cornstarch
spoon

Procedure

- Pour 8 tablespoons (120 ml) of water into the bowl.
- Slowly add the cornstarch to the water. Stir well after each addition. NOTE: *The mixture should be so thick that it is very hard to stir.* Add a few drops of water if all of the starch will not dissolve or a little starch if the mixture looks thin.
- Place your hand on the surface of the mixture in the bowl and very gently push downward.
- When your hand has sunk into the mixture try to lift your hand out of the bowl.

Results Your hand slowly sinks into the cornstarch mixture, but cannot be pulled out easily. The bowl rises as you lift your hand.

Why? A non-Newtonian fluid is a material whose **viscosity** (thickness) increases when pressure is applied to it. Pushing or pulling on the mixture makes it so thick and firm that it is difficult to pull your hand out.

98. Magnesium Milk?

Purpose To make a milky, magnesia solution.

Materials   1 small baby-food jar
distilled water
1 teaspoon (5 ml) Epsom salts
2 teaspoons (10 ml) household
   ammonia
Adult helper

Procedure

- Fill the jar ½ full with water.
- Stir the Epsom salts into the water.
- Ask your adult helper to pour the ammonia into the jar. *DO NOT STIR.*

CAUTION: *Handle the ammonia with care and work in a well-ventilated area. Ammonia is poisonous, and its fumes can damage skin and the mucous membranes of the nose, mouth, and eyes.*

- Allow the solution to stand for 5 minutes.

Results A white, milky substance forms as the ammonia mixes with the Epsom salts solution.

Why? Household ammonia's chemical name is ammonium hydroxide. Magnesium sulfate is the chemical name for Epsom salts. Mixing ammonia and Epsom salts causes a chemical change that produces magnesium hydroxide. Magnesium hydroxide is a white substance that does not dissolve well in water. After standing awhile, the white floating particles settle to the bottom of the jar.

CAUTION: *It is not safe to drink the magnesium hydroxide made in this experiment. The medicine known as Milk of Magnesia is a suspension of magnesium hydroxide in water.*

99. Testing for Starch

Purpose To test for the presence of starch in different materials.

Materials Testing Samples:
      notebook paper
      cheese
      bread
      cracker
      sugar
      apple slice
    baking sheet
    Tincture of Iodine
    eyedropper
    adult helper

Procedure
- Place the testing samples on the cookie sheet. CAUTION: *Keep the iodine out of reach of small children. It is poisonous and is for external use only. It stains clothes and skin.*
- Ask an adult to place one drop of iodine on each of the testing samples.
- Observe where the iodine touches the samples.
- Discard the samples.

Results The paper, bread, and cracker turn a dark blue-purple. The other samples are just stained by the brown iodine solution.

Why? Starch combines with iodine to form a dark blue-purple compound. Only the samples containing starch turn dark blue-purple where the iodine is added.

100. Limestone Deposits

Purpose To collect limestone and then, chemically remove it.

Materials small baby-food jar
    limewater (prepared in Experiment 118)
    vinegar

Procedure
- Fill the jar with limewater.
- Leave the jar open and allow it to sit undisturbed for seven days.
- Pour out the limewater.
- Observe the white crust around the inside of the jar.
- Fill the jar ½ full with vinegar.
- Watch the changes that occur.

Results A white crust covers the inside of the jar. The material in the white deposit reacts with the vinegar to produce bubbles. Large pieces of the crust fall away from the walls of the jar and dissolve in the vinegar. Within 5 minutes the glass touched by the vinegar is clear. The crust not touched by the vinegar remains on the glass.

Why? Carbon dioxide in the air mixes with the limewater and forms the white crust called limestone.

Limestone has the chemical name of calcium carbonate. When calcium carbonate is mixed with vinegar, a reaction takes place in which calcium carbonate is changed and bubbles of carbon dioxide are produced.

101. A Different Form

Purpose To produce a different form of matter.

Materials   1 teaspoon (5 ml) baking soda
1-quart (1-liter) plastic soda bottle
3 tablespoons (45 ml) vinegar
1 18-inch (2.3-cm) balloon
cellophane tape

Procedure
- Pour the baking soda into the bottle.
- Pour the vinegar into the balloon.
- Attach the open end of the balloon to the mouth of the bottle. Use the tape to secure the balloon to the bottle.
- Raise the balloon to allow the vinegar to pour into the bottle.

Results The mixture starts to bubble and the balloon inflates.

Why? A chemical change occurs when the vinegar and baking soda mix together. The balloon inflates because it becomes filled with the carbon dioxide gas produced. The starting materials were in the solid and liquid form, and one of the products from the reaction is in the gas form.

102. Hard Water

Purpose To determine what makes water hard.

Materials   2 baby-food jars with lids
distilled water
½ teaspoon (2.5 ml) Epsom salts
spoon
eyedropper
dishwashing liquid

Procedure
- Fill both jars ½ full with distilled water.
- To one jar of water, add the Epsom salts. Stir well.
- Add 3 drops of dishwashing liquid to each jar.
- Secure the lids on the jars.
- Shake the jars vigorously back and forth 15 times.
- Allow the jar to stand for 10 seconds.
- Observe and describe the appearance of the suds.

Results Soapsuds form in both jars, but they rise higher in the jar without the Epsom salts.

Why? Saying that water is "hard" does not mean that it is a solid, but that it contains calcium, magnesium, and/or iron salts. Epsom salt is a magnesium salt. Water without these salts is called "soft." Hard water does not make suds as well as soft water because the salts and the soap chemically react, forming a slimy film called **soap scum**.

103. Colder Water

Purpose To lower the temperature of icy water.

Materials 1 small, metal can
crushed ice
tap water
outdoor thermometer
timer
1 tablespoon (15 ml) table salt

Procedure
- Fill the can with crushed ice.
- Cover the ice with water.
- Insert the thermometer.
- Wait 30 seconds and record the temperature.
- Add 1 tablespoon (15 ml) of table salt to the icy water and stir very gently with the thermometer.
- Wait 30 seconds and record the temperature.

Results The temperature lowers when the salt is added.

Why? It takes energy for the salt crystals to break apart into tiny particles small enough to **dissolve** in the water. This needed energy is obtained by removing heat from the water, which causes the water to be colder.

104. Growing Ice

Purpose To demonstrate that water expands when frozen.

Materials clay, a piece the size of a marble
1 small baby-food jar
tap water
blue food coloring
spoon
1 straw
permanent marking pen

Procedure
- Press the piece of clay against the inside bottom of the jar.
- Fill the jar with water.
- Add 10 drops of food coloring and stir.
- Slowly lower the straw into the colored water.
- Push the bottom of the straw into the clay. The straw can now stand in a vertical position.
- Slowly pour all of the water out of the jar.
- Use the pen to mark the height of the water in the straw.
- Place the jar in a freezer overnight.

Results The height of the frozen water is above the mark.

Why? Water molecules are attracted to one another, and when they get close enough they bond, or stick, together. They do not stack together like flat boxes, but have spaces between them. Liquid water molecules occupy less volume because, at the higher temperature, the molecules are more flexible and can crowd together. As the temperature lowers, the molecules bond together to form a hexagonal structure. This ice structure is not very flexible and takes up more space than the same number of liquid water molecules.

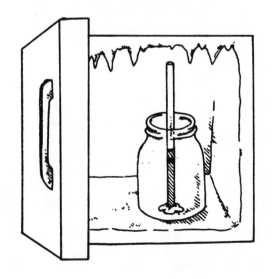

105. Needles

Purpose To grow needle-shaped crystals of Epsom salts.

Materials   1 small baby-food jar
tap water
2 tablespoons (30 ml) Epsom salts
spoon
scissors
1 sheet of dark construction paper
saucer

Procedure

- Fill the jar ½ full with water.
- Add the Epsom salts to the water. Stir.
- Cut a circle from the construction paper to fit the inside of the saucer.
- Pour a thin layer of the salt solution over the paper. Try not to pour out the undissolved salt.
- Place the saucer in a warm place and wait several days.

Results Long, slender, needle-shaped crystals form on the paper.

Why? Epsom salt crystals are long and slender. The particles in the box have been crushed for packaging

and do not have a slender shape. As the water **evaporates** from the solution, small, unseen crystals start to stack together. Further evaporation increases the building process and long, needle-shaped crystals are produced.

106. Lace

Purpose To grow a layer of lacy salt crystals.

Materials   measuring cup
tap water
tall, slender, clear jar
3 tablespoons (45 ml) table salt
spoon
scissors
ruler
black construction paper

Procedure

- Pour ½ cup (250 ml) water into the jar.
- Add the salt and stir.
- Cut a ½-inch strip from the construction paper. The height of the paper should be about one-half the height of the jar.
- Stand the paper strip against the inside of the jar.
- Place the jar in a visible place where it will be undisturbed.
- Allow the jar to sit for 3 to 4 weeks. Observe it daily.

Results Lacy crystals may be seen at the top and sides of the paper after several days. More lace develops the longer the jar sits.

Why? The salty water moves up the paper and onto the glass where it spreads out. The water **evaporates** leaving microscopic bits of salt on the glass. This continues until visible crystals of salt are seen. The water continues to evaporate, producing layers of lacy crystals around the inside of the jar.

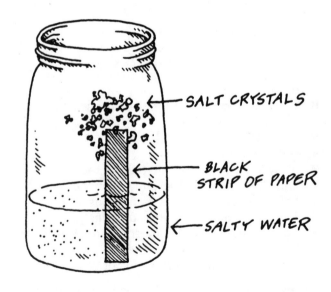

SALT CRYSTALS

BLACK STRIP OF PAPER

SALTY WATER

107. Soakers

Purpose To compare the water-absorbing ability of paper diapers and cloth diapers.

Materials 2 2-quart (2-liter) bowls
tap water
paper diaper
baking pan
cloth diaper
timer
ruler

Procedure

NOTE: *Dispose of the paper diaper material in the trash. Do not put any of the material down the drain.*

- Fill both bowls with water. Be sure the water levels are the same in both bowls.
- Place the paper diaper in one of the bowls.
- Hold the diaper under the water for 10 seconds. Lift the diaper and place it on the baking pan.
- Place the cloth diaper in the second bowl.
- Hold the diaper under the water for 10 seconds, lift and place it on the baking pan.
- Compare the level of the water left in each of the bowls by holding a ruler upright inside first one bowl, then the other.

Results The water level is lower in the bowl that held the paper diaper.

Why? The paper diaper contains a chemical called sodium polyacrylate. This chemical can **absorb** (take in or swallow up) large amounts of water. Thus, paper diapers with sodium polyacrylate are more absorbant than cloth diapers without the chemical.

108. Streamers of Color

Purpose To observe how solute dissolves in a solvent.

Materials clear drinking glass
tap water
flat toothpick
powdered fruit drink (Select a fruit drink that has a dark color such as cherry, grape, or raspberry.)

Procedure

- Fill the glass with water.
- Use the wide end of a flat toothpick to pick up some of the powdered drink.
- Gently shake the powder over the glass of water.
- Observe from the side of the glass.
- Continue to add the powder until the water becomes completely colored.

Results Streams of color descend through the water.

Why? The crystals **dissolve** in the water as they fall. Dissolving means that a dissolving material breaks apart into smaller and smaller particles and spreads evenly throughout the solvent. The dissolving material, the **solute**, is the powdered crystals and the **solvent** is the water. The combination of a solute and a solvent produces a liquid solution.

109. Speedy Soup

Purpose To show how temperature affects how long it takes for a material to dissolve.

Materials 2 cups
warm and cold tap water
2 bouillon cubes
spoon

Procedure
- Fill one cup with cold tap water.
- Add one bouillon cube.
- Allow this cup to sit undisturbed while the second cup is prepared.
- Fill the second cup with warm tap water.
- Add one bouillon cube to the water and stir.

Results The solid cube dissolved more quickly when placed in warm water and stirred.

Why? Dissolving means that the **solute** breaks apart and moves evenly throughout the **solvent**. The bouillon cube is the solute and the water the solvent. Heat causes the molecules of water to move faster, thus the water molecules hit the cube, causing pieces to break off. Stirring increases the breaking process. The cube will finally dissolve in the cold water, but it takes a much longer period of time. Stirring the cold water will help speed up the dissolving.

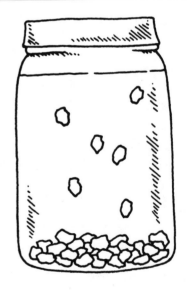

110. Falling Snow

Purpose To produce a miniature snow storm.

Materials 3 tablespoons (45 ml) boric acid crystals (available at a drugstore)
large baby-food jar with lid
tap water

Procedure
- Pour the boric acid crystals into the glass jar.
- Fill the jar to overflowing with water.
- Screw the lid on tightly.
- Shake the jar to mix the crystals and water, then allow the jar to stand undisturbed.

Results Some of the crystals dissolve in the water, but most of them float to the bottom like snowflakes.

Why? Boric acid does not **dissolve** well in water. It takes only a few crystals to form a saturated boric acid solution. A **saturated solution** is one in which no more solute will dissolve at a specific tempeature. Shaking the jar causes the undissolved crystals to float around and then **gravity** pulls them to the bottom of the jar.

111. Strengths?

Purpose To compare the strengths of tea.

Materials 2 cups
tap water
teaspoon (5 ml)
instant tea

Procedure
- Fill the cups with water.
- Add ¼ teaspoon (1.3 ml) of instant tea to one cup and stir.
- Add 1 heaping teaspoon (5 ml) of instant tea to the second cup and stir.
- Observe the color of the tea solution in each cup.

Results One of the solutions is lighter in color.

Why? Solutions are liquid mixtures made of a **solute** and a **solvent**. The solute is the substance being dissolved and the solvent is doing the dissolving. In the tea solutions, tea is the solute and water the solvent. The lighter colored solution has less solute than the darker colored solution and is said to be weak or **diluted**. The darker solution with the greater amount of solute is strong or **concentrated**.

DILUTE, WEAK, LIGHT

CONCENTRATED, STRONG, DARK

112. Layering

Purpose To observe layering of undissolved materials.

Materials 2 tablespoons (30 ml) of any large dried bean
2 tablespoons (30 ml) flour
quart (liter) glass jar with a lid
tap water

Procedure
- Place the beans and flour in the jar.
- Fill the jar with water.
- Screw the lid on tightly.
- Shake the jar to mix all the materials thoroughly.
- Let the jar stand undisturbed for 20 minutes.
- Observe.

Results The beans settle first with a fine layer of flour on top.

Why? The beans and flour are not capable of being dissolved in the water. As soon as the shaking stops, **gravity** starts pulling these undissolved materials down. The heavier beans settle first. The tiny flour particles remain suspended in the water for a few minutes, but finally are pulled to the bottom of the jar.

A mixture containing particles suspended in a liquid that usually settles on standing is called a **suspension**. Water in a fast-flowing stream forms a suspension by picking up rocks and soil that temporarily stay suspended in the moving water, but the materials settle out in layers on the stream bed, as did the beans and flour, when the water's speed is reduced.

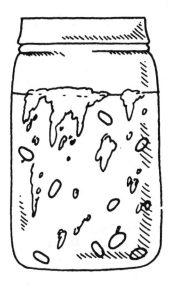

113. Spinning

Purpose To separate the suspended parts of a suspension by spinning.

Materials hammer
nail
1-lb. metal coffee can
3 feet (1 m) cotton twine
tap water
2 tablespoons (30 ml) flour
clear drinking glass
adult helper

Procedure

- Ask an adult to use the hammer and nail to make two holes across from each other beneath the top rim of the can.
- Tie the ends of the twine in these holes.
- Fill the can ½ full with water.
- Stir the flour into the water.
- Carry the can and the empty glass outside.
- Hold the twine and swing the can around 15 times.
CAUTION: *Stand in an open area. Do not release the twine.*
- Pour a small amount of the liquid into the empty glass. If it looks cloudy, swing 10 more times.

- Continue to swing and test for cloudiness until the liquid stops changing.

Results The solution clears.

Why? The mixture of the flour and water forms a **suspension**. As soon as the stirring stops, the undissolved flour particles start settling to the bottom of the can. Spinning the can produces a strong outward force. This force pushes the suspended flour particles to the bottom of the can. Thus, spinning the can speeds the settling process.

114. Spicy Perfume

Purpose To make a bottle of spicy perfume.

Materials 15 whole cloves
small baby-food jar with lid
rubbing alcohol

Procedure

CAUTION: *Do not get alcohol near your nose or mouth.*
- Place the whole cloves in the jar.
- Fill the jar ½ full with the rubbing alcohol.
- Secure the lid and allow the jar to set for seven days.
- Use your finger to dab a few drops of the liquid on your wrist.
- Wait about 15 seconds to allow the alcohol to evaporate, then smell your wrist.

Results The skin has a faint, spicy smell.

Why? The alcohol **dissolves** the aromatic oil in the cloves. When the alcohol **evaporates** from the wrist, the scented oil is left on the skin. Perfumes are made by dissolving oils from flowers and other aromatic materials in alcohol.

115. Smoke Rings

Purpose To observe the downward flow of cold colored water through warmer clear water.

Materials 1 ice cube
small baby-food jar
1 large-mouthed, clear, glass, quart (liter) jar
warm and cold tap water
eyedropper
red food coloring
6-inch (15-cm) square aluminum foil
rubber band
pencil

Procedure

- Place the ice cube in the baby-food jar. Fill the jar with cold water.
- Fill the quart jar to within an inch of the top with warm tap water.
- Remove the ice cube from the baby-food jar. Add and stir in 6 to 7 drops of food coloring.
- Cover the mouth of the baby-food jar with aluminum foil. Use the rubber band to secure the foil around the mouth of the jar.
- Use the point of a pencil to make a small hole in the aluminum foil.

- Quickly turn the baby-food jar upside down and hold it so that the hole is just beneath the surface of the warm water.
- Slowly and gently tap the bottom of the baby-food jar with your finger.

Results The cold colored water flows downward. The tapping causes the colored water to come out in spurts, producing smoke-like rings of color in the warm clear water.

Why? The molecules of water, like all matter, are spaced closer together when cold and farther apart when heated. Thus, each drop of cold water has more water molecules and is heavier than a drop of warmer water. Since the cold water is heavier, it sinks down through the warmer water. The food coloring has little effect on the **weight** of the cold water.

116. Melt Down

Purpose To determine the effect that color has on the amount of light that an object absorbs.

Materials 2 ice cubes of equal size
2 plastic sandwich bags that zip closed
2 sheets of construction paper, one black and one white
timer

Procedure

- Place one ice cube in each of the plastic bags. Close the bags.
- Lay the bags on a table outside and in a sunny area.
- Cover each bag with one of the pieces of paper.
- Lift the pieces of paper every 5 minutes for 30 minutes and observe the ice cube in each bag.

Results The ice covered by the black paper melted faster.

Why? Light is a form of energy. Black objects **absorb** more light energy than do white objects so the temperature under the black sheet of paper is higher. The ice cube melted faster because the temperature was higher under the black paper.

117. Phenol Who?

Purpose To make a basic indicator called phenolphthalein.

Materials   4 tablespoons (60 ml) rubbing alcohol
2 baby-food jars—one with a lid
1 tablet Ex-Lax®
CAUTION: *Ex-Lax is a medicine. Do not eat.*
spoon
marking pen
masking tape
adult helper

Procedure

CAUTION: *Keep alcohol away from your nose and mouth.*

- Pour the rubbing alcohol into one jar.
- Ask an adult to add broken pieces of the Ex-Lax tablet.
- Use the spoon to crush and stir the tablet pieces.
- All of the tablet will not dissolve. Allow the jar to stand undisturbed for 5 minutes until all the undissolved pieces settle to the bottom. Pour the clearer liquid at the top into the second jar.

- Use the marking pen and tape to label this jar "phenolphthalein."
- Secure the lid to store.
- Keep the phenolphthalein for further testing in the next experiment.

Results A clear liquid is separated from the brown pieces.

Why? The alcohol **dissolves** the chemical called **phenolphthalein** that is in the laxative. This chemical turns bright pink when mixed with a **base** (a chemical containing hydroxide ions). Phenolphthalein is an **indicator** (a dye that changes color in the presence of an acid or base) that can be used to test for the presence of hydroxide ions. (Keep your phenolphthalein for further testing in the next experiment.)

118. Pink!

Purpose To observe the effect that acids and bases have on phenolphthalein.

Materials   2 quart (liter) jars, 1 lid
distilled water
measuring spoons
pickling lime (found in store with food canning supplies)
masking tape
marking pen
2 small baby-food jars
white vinegar
1 eyedropper
phenolphthalein (see Experiment 117)
adult helper

Procedure

- Ask an adult to prepare limewater by filling one quart (liter) jar three-fourths full with distilled water. Add ¼ teaspoon (1.25 ml) of lime. Stir and allow to stand overnight. Pour the clear liquid into the second quart (liter) jar. Be careful not to pour out any of the lime that has settled on the bottom.
- Put on the lid securely, use tape and the marking pen to label the jar LIMEWATER, and keep for following experiments.

CAUTION: *Do not get lime in your nose, mouth, or eyes.*

- Fill one small jar ¼ full with vinegar, and with the tape and marking pen, label it ACID.
- Fill a second jar one-fourth full with limewater, label it BASE.
- With the eyedropper, add three drops of phenolphthalein to the jar of acid and to the jar of base.
- Swirl the liquid in each jar to mix.
- Observe any color change in the jars.

Results The color of the acid is unchanged, but the base turns a bright pink.

Why? Indicators are chemicals that make a specific color change in an acid or a base. **Phenolphthalein** is an indicator for a **base**. The color change is from clear to bright pink in a base, but there is no color change with an **acid**.

119. Basic Cleaner

Purpose To test for the presence of a base in a common cleanser.

Materials ¼ cup (63 ml) rubbing alcohol
¼ teaspoon (1.25 ml) turmeric powder (a spice)
quart (liter) bowl
spoon
5 large coffee filters
tweezers
cookie sheet
scissors
zip-lock plastic bag
measuring spoon
powdered abrasive cleanser
tap water

Procedure

CAUTION: *Keep alcohol away from your nose and mouth.*

■ Make a basic testing paper by mixing the alcohol and turmeric together in the bowl. Dip the coffee filters into the turmeric solution one at a time. Use the tweezers to lift each filter out of the bowl and place on the cookie sheet. Allow the filters to dry.

■ Cut the dry papers into strips about ½ × 4 inches (1.25 × 10 cm) and store in the plastic bag. (Save for the next experiment.)
■ In a cup mix together 1 tablespoon (15 ml) of powdered cleanser and 3 tablespoons (45 ml) of water.
■ Dip the end of a turmeric strip in the solution.

Results The yellow paper turns red where it touches the solution.

Why? Bases turn turmeric from yellow to red. Because bases combine with grease to form soap, most cleansers contain basic chemicals. The cleanser reacts with unwanted grease and the soap that is formed is washed away easily.

120. Neutral

Purpose To neutralize a basic solution.

Materials aluminum foil, 6 × 6 inch (15 × 15 cm)
turmeric strip (prepared in Experiment 119)
2 eyedroppers
limewater (prepared in Experiment 118)
vinegar

Procedure

■ Place the aluminum foil on a table and lay one turmeric strip in the center.
■ Add two drops of limewater to the end of the turmeric strip.
■ Fill the second eyedropper with vinegar.
■ Add two drops of vinegar on the same end of the turmeric strip.

Results Limewater turns the turmeric paper red. The vinegar drops change the red color of the paper back to yellow.

Why? Limewater is a **base** and vinegar is an **acid**. The combination of an acid and a base produce new chemicals that are not acidic or basic. The basic lime-

water causes the turmeric paper to turn red. The drops of vinegar remove the basic limewater by changing it to a nonbasic chemical.

IV
Earth Science

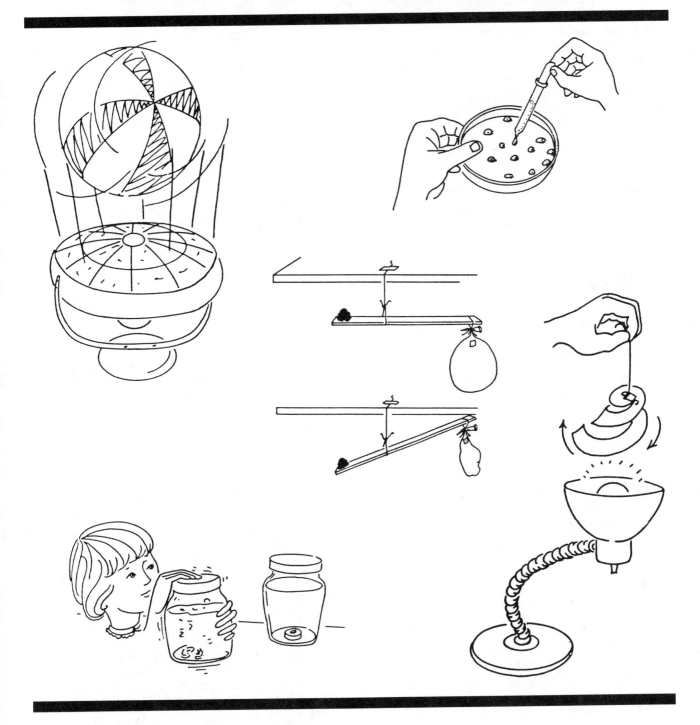

121. Tilt

Purpose To demonstrate the effect of the Earth's tilt on seasons.

Materials 2 pencils
ball of modeling clay the size of an apple
flashlight

Procedure

- Insert a pencil through the ball of clay.
- Use the second pencil to mark the equator line around the center of the clay ball. This line should be halfway between the top and bottom of the ball.
- Position the ball on a table so that the pencil eraser is leaning slightly to the right.
- In a darkened room, place the flashlight about 6 inches (15 cm) from the left side of the ball.
- Observe where the light strikes the ball.
- Place the light about 6 inches (15 cm) from the right side of the clay ball.
- Observe where the light strikes the ball.

Results The area below the equator receives the most light when the pencil eraser points away from the light, and the area above the equator is brighter when the pencil eraser points toward the light.

Why? The pencil represents the imaginary axis running through the Earth. The Northern Hemisphere, the area above the equator, is warmed the most when the Earth's axis points toward the Sun. This is because more direct light rays hit the area. The Southern Hemisphere, the area below the equator, receives the warming direct light rays when the Earth's axis points away from the Sun. The direction of the Earth's axis changes very slightly during the Earth's movement around the Sun, causing the Southern and Northern Hemispheres to receive different amounts of light rays. This results in a change of seasons.

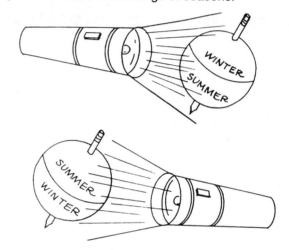

122. Rotation

Purpose To demonstrate that the Earth rotates.

Materials 2-liter soda bottle   string
masking tape   outdoor swing set
sand   dark colored
scissors   poster board
ruler   adult helper

Procedure

- Ask an adult helper to punch a hole in the bottom of the bottle about the size of a pencil's diameter.
- Place a piece of tape over the hole.
- Fill the bottle about ¾ full with sand.
- Cut a 24-inch (60-cm) piece of string and tie each end around the neck of the bottle, forming a loop.
- Cut a second string, about 6 inches (15 cm) taller than the swing set, and tie it to the loop around the bottle.
- Lay the poster board on the ground under the swing set.
- Wrap the swings around the side poles of the swing set so they are out of the way.
- Hold the bottle about 2 inches (5 cm) above the paper while your adult helper ties the free end of the shorter string to the top bar of the swing set.

- Remove the tape from the hole and start the bottle moving in a wide swing.
- Observe the pattern of the sand on the paper.

Results The path of the swinging bottle changes.

Why? Actually the swinging bottle changes its direction very little, but because the Earth rotates the ground underneath the bottle moved. The hanging bottle represents a Foucault's pendulum, named after physicist Jean Foucault who first performed the experiment in 1851.

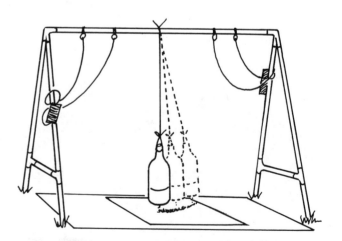

123. Deposits

Purpose To demonstrate the formation of caliche deposits.

Materials 1 quart (liter), large-mouthed jar
distilled water
measuring spoons
pickling lime (found with food canning supplies)
masking tape
marking pen
adult helper

Procedure
- Fill the jar ½ full with water.
- Ask an adult to add ½ teaspoon (2.5 ml) of lime to the water and stir.
CAUTION: *Keep lime away from your eyes, nose, and mouth.*
- Place a piece of tape down the side of the jar.
- Mark the height of the liquid in the jar with the marking pen.
- Place the jar where it will remain undisturbed.
- Observe the jar daily for 2 weeks.

Results The water level drops, and a white crusty deposit forms above the water line on the inside of the jar.

Why? Like the jar of limewater, ground water contains large amounts of minerals, including calcium. When carbon dioxide gas from the air dissolves in the mineral water, a white solid called calcium carbonate is formed. As the water **evaporates**, a crust of white calcium carbonate is left. Large deposits of calcium carbonate are found in the semi-arid southwestern United States. These deposits, known as **caliche**, are found on or near the surface of the ground.

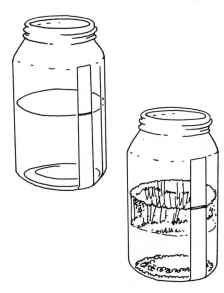

124. Splitter

Purpose To determine how ice can split rocks.

Materials small plastic bowl with a tight-fitting lid
cold tap water

Procedure
- Fill the plastic bowl to over flowing with water.
- Secure the lid.
- Place the closed container in the freezer.
- After 24 hours remove the bowl.

Results The water has frozen, expanded, and pushed the lid off the bowl.

Why? Most substances expand when heated and contract when cooled. Water molecules are attracted to each other, forming a flexible chain. This ability to twist around allows liquid water molecules to crowd into smaller spaces. When the water freezes the ice structure that forms is solid and takes up more space than the same number of liquid water molecules. When water seeps into cracks in rocks and freezes the expanding ice can push hard enough to break the rocks apart.

125. Spoon Pen

Purpose To demonstrate a mineral streak test.

Materials metal spoon (stainless steel)
unglazed porcelain tile (The back of any porcelain tile will work.)

Procedure
- Rub the handle of the spoon across the back of the porcelain tile.
- Write your name on the back of the tile with the spoon handle.

Results The spoon makes a dark grey mark on the white tile.

Why? A streak test is made by rubbing a mineral sample across a piece of unglazed porcelain. The color of the streak made is the same as the color of the powdered mineral. Grinding the spoon into a powder would produce the same dark grey color as is seen on the porcelain streak plate. The color of the streak made by a mineral can be an important clue in identifying the mineral.

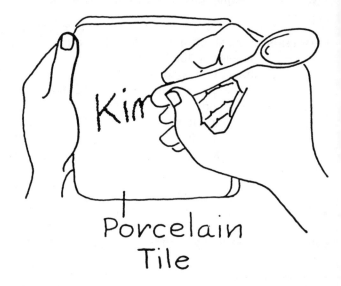

126. Sampler

Purpose To demonstrate core sampling.

Materials 3 different colors of modeling clay
drinking straw
fingernail scissors

Procedure
- Soften an egg-sized piece of each color of clay by squeezing it in your hands.
- Flatten the clay pieces, and stack them on top of each other to form a block about 1 inch (2.5 cm) deep.
- Push the straw through the layers of clay.
- Pull the tube out of the clay.
- Use the scissors to cut open the straw.
- Remove the clay plug.

Results The straw cuts a cylinder-shaped sample from the layered stack of clay.

Why? As the straw cuts through the clay, the clay is pushed up inside the hollow tube. The captured clay is called a core sample, and it reveals what materials are layered inside the block of clay. Coring devises made of metal are used to cut through layers of soil just as the layers of clay were cut. The metal core sampler has a plunger that pushes the soil out so that it can be studied.

127. Sinkers

Purpose To demonstrate how placer ore deposits form.

Materials quart (liter) glass jar with lid
tap water
1 cup (250 ml) soil
5 paper clips

Procedure
- Fill the jar ½ full with water.
- Add the soil and paper clips.
- Close the lid and shake the jar vigorously.
- Allow the jar to stand undisturbed for 5 minutes.

Results The paper clips fall quickly to the bottom of the jar, and the slower-moving soil settles on top of the clips.

Why? Most of the soil falls more slowly than the heavier paper clips, and thus a layer of soil forms on top of the paper clips. In nature, rain beats on top of the soil, shaking and softening it. The heavier materials in this wet mixture sink lower and lower as the years pass. Heavy grains of metal continue to sink until they reach a hard rock layer. Particles of metal that combine in this method are called **placer ore** deposits.

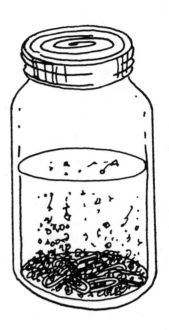

128. Prints

Purpose To determine how fossils were preserved.

Materials
modeling clay   plastic spoon
paper plate   plaster of paris
seashell   tap water
petroleum jelly   paper cup

Procedure
- Place a piece of clay about the size of a lemon on the paper plate.
- Rub the outside of the seashell with petroleum jelly.
- Press the seashell into clay.
- Carefully remove the seashell so that a clear imprint of the shell remains in the clay.
- Mix 4 spoons of plaster of paris with 2 spoons of water in the paper cup and do not wash any plaster down the sink. It can clog the drain.
- Pour the plaster mixture into the imprint in the clay. Throw the paper cup and spoon away.
- Allow the plaster to harden, about 15 to 20 minutes.
- Separate the clay from the plaster mold.

Results The clay has an imprint of the outside of the shell, and the plaster looks like the outside of the shell.

Why? The layer of clay and the plaster are both examples of **fossils** (any impression or trace of organisms from past geologic times). The clay represents the soft mud of ancient times. Organisms made imprints in the mud. If nothing collected in the prints, the mud dried, forming what is now called a cast fossil. When sediments filled the imprint, a sedimentary rock formed with the print of the organism on the outside. This type of fossil is called a mold fossil.

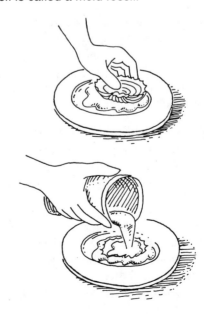

129. Rub-A-Dub

Purpose To demonstrate the effect of heat produced by crustal movement.

Materials scissors
cardboard
glass soda bottle
refrigerator
1 cup (250 ml) tap water

Procedure
- Cut a circle from the cardboard that is slightly larger than the top of the bottle.
- Place the empty bottle in the freezer for 20 minutes.
- Remove the bottle from the freezer.
- Dip the cardboard into the cup of water and place it over the mouth of the bottle.
- Quickly rub the palms of your hands together about 20 times.
- Immediately place your hands around the outside of the bottle.

Results One side of the cardboard circle rises and falls.

Why? Molecules that move and collide emit heat energy. Rubbing your hands together produces heat, and this heat causes the cold air in the bottle to warm up and expand. This expanded gas pushes up on the paper with enough force to partially lift the paper and allow the hot gas to escape. When sections of the Earth's crust rub against each other as they move, the heat produced causes the rock material to vibrate. If molecules in the solid rock move fast enough, they break away from each other, and the solid melts into **magma** (liquid rock beneath the ground). Further heating can cause the liquid to change into a gas. Most materials become larger when heated. Crustal changes such as earthquakes and volcanos occur when materials inside the earth expand, forcing materials out through the Earth's surface.

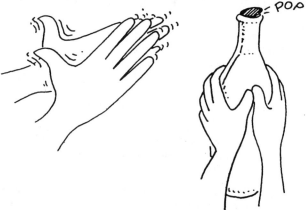

130. Stretch

Purpose To demonstrate the effect of a tension force.

Materials balloon
marking pen

Procedure
- Draw a square on a deflated balloon.
- Divide the square into three sections.
- Use the marking pen to color the two outer sections on the square.
- Inflate the balloon and observe the markings.
- Deflate the balloon and observe the markings again.

Results The square spreads out in all directions when the balloon is inflated. If the balloon has not been inflated too much, it will recover its original shape and size when deflated.

Why? The rubber molecules of the balloon are being pulled apart by the pressure of the air inside. Parts of the balloon stretch more than others, causing a change in the shape of the diagram drawn on the rubber. **Tension** is a stretching or pulling-apart force. If the force is not too great, rocks with elastic properties like the balloon will recover their original shape and size when the force is removed. If the force is too strong, the rocks cannot remain together, and they break apart—as the balloon would if you continued to inflate it with air. When there is an earthquake, the rocks in the Earth's crust are pushed apart by this force.

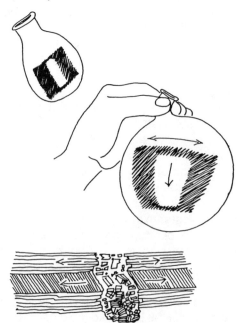

131. Flowing Ice

Purpose To determine one of the ways that glaciers might move.

Materials square cake pan
tap water
a freezer
a wire rack
a brick, or any object of comparable
size and weight

Procedure
- Fill the cake pan with water.
- Place the pan in the freezer until the water is frozen solid.
- Remove the ice from the pan and set the ice block on the wire rack in the freezer.
- Lay the brick on top of the ice block.
- Observe the bottom of the ice block after 24 hours.

Results The ice moves through the spaces between the wire rack.

Why? **Glaciers** are large masses of ice in motion. When the pressure builds up on the bottom layer, it melts and becomes soft and pliable. The melting of ice due to pressure and its subsequent refreezing is called **regelation**. This softer ice moves outward like thick honey. As long as snow continues to fall on the surface, the height of the glacier remains constant and fingers of ice move out from the bottom of the mountain of ice. Some glaciers move only a few inches (cm) each day, while others move many yards (m) in a single day.

132. Spurt

Purpose To demonstrate what causes magma (liquid rock) to move.

Materials ½-empty tube of toothpaste

Procedure
- Hold the tube of toothpaste in your hands.
- With the cap screwed on tight, press against the tube with your thumbs and fingers.
- Move your fingers and press in different places on the tube.

Results The paste in the tube moves out from under your fingers. Toothpaste bulges around the sides of your fingers.

Why? Liquid rock inside the earth is called **magma.** Pressure on pools of magma deep within the Earth forces the molten rock toward the surface. Magma cools and hardens as it rises toward the surface. The liquid moves into the closest open space as did the toothpaste when it squeezed between and around the spaces formed by your fingers. Magma that moves up vertically into cracks in the crust and hardens is called a **dike.** When magma moves horizontally between rock layers, the solid, thin sheet of rock formed is called a **sill.** This horizontal movement of magma can also form a pool of liquid. This hardened dome-shaped pool is called a **laccolith.** As the laccolith forms, the layers of rock above it are pushed up, just as the toothpaste was pushed up the tube.

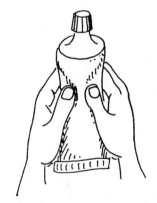

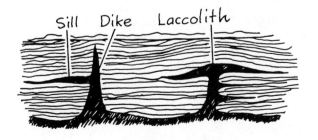

133. Rusty Rock

Purpose To demonstrate how oxygen causes a rock to crumble.

Materials steel wool without soap (found in paint department)
tap water
saucer

Procedure
- Use a piece of steel wool about the size of a lemon.
- Moisten the steel wool with water and place it on the saucer.
- Allow it to sit in the saucer for 3 days.
- Pick up the steel wool after 3 days and rub it between your fingers.

CAUTION: *Steel wool can give splinters. You may want to wear a rubber glove.*

Results Parts of the steel wool seem to have turned into a red powder.

Why? Oxygen combines with the iron in the steel wool pad, forming iron oxide, or rust. Rocks with streaks of yellow, orange, or reddish-brown usually contain iron. The iron at the surface of the rock forms iron oxide when exposed to moist air and eventually crumbles away as did the steel wool.

134. Rub Away

Purpose To demonstrate how rocks change into sand and thin soil.

Materials writing paper
pencil with eraser

Procedure
- Write your name on the paper with the pencil.
- Rub the eraser back and forth over the writing.

Results The writing is removed and small particles are left on the paper.

Why? Graphite is a mineral found in many rocks. Pencil erasers are made of high-friction materials. Pushing this material across the soft graphite markings left by the pencil rubs the particles of graphite and some of the paper off and also much of the eraser. When wind blows sand particles against rocks, the grinding of the sand against the rocks acts like the eraser and removes small pieces of the rock. Over a period of time, more and more of the rock is rubbed away, and instead of a solid rock, only sand and thin soil are left.

135. Break Down

Purpose To demonstrate how water, with and without sediment in it, wears away a solid.

Materials 3 tablespoons (45 ml) dirt
small glass bowl
spoon
white school glue
paper towel
2 plastic bowls of equal size with lids
tap water
1 teaspoon (5 ml) aquarium gravel

Procedure

- Place the dirt in the bowl.
- Stir in enough glue to make a stiff mixture.
- Shape the mixture into two balls of equal size.
- Wipe the glass bowl clean with a paper towel and place the balls of dirt inside the bowl.
- Place the glass bowl in a sunny area and allow the dirt balls to harden for several days.
- Fill each plastic bowl half full with water.
- Add the gravel to one of the plastic bowls.
- Place one dirt ball in each bowl and secure the lid.
- Shake each bowl vigorously 10 times.

- Open the lids and observe the shape of each dirt ball.
- Close the lid. Shake and observe three more times.

Results The shape of both balls changes, but the ball in the bowl with the gravel changes faster.

Why? Land can be worn down by moving water. This change in the land is called **weathering** (the breaking and wearing away of rocks and other land features). The dirt balls (homemade rocks) in the bowls were weathered by the water and bowl hitting against them. The gravel sped up the weathering process by scraping against the surface of the dirt ball.

136. Pile Up

Purpose To demonstrate how sand dunes are formed.

Materials shallow baking pan
flour
meat baster

Procedure

- Cover the bottom of the baking pan with a thin, flat layer of flour.
- Use your hand to support the baster with its open end about 2 inches (5 cm) from the edge of the flour.
- Squeeze the bulb of the baster 10 times.

Results The flour moves away from the end of the baster in a semicircular pattern. The flour piles up close to the end of the baster.

Why? The moving air leaving the baster has **kinetic energy** (energy of motion). The flour particles are small enough to be lifted by the moving air and carried forward. Some of the smaller particles move farther away, but most lose energy and fall, forming a mound near the end of the baster. As this mound builds, it blocks the movement of even the smaller

flour particles that would have traveled farther. This demonstrates how sand dunes are formed.

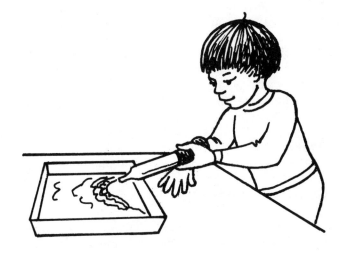

137. Shake-Up

Purpose To determine the effect of motion on weathering.

Materials measuring cup (250 ml)
tap water
2 equal-sized jars with lids
2 equal-sized pieces of colored hard candy

Procedure
- Pour 1 cup (250 ml) of water into each jar.
- Add 1 piece of candy to each jar and close the jar with a lid.
- Place one jar where it will not be disturbed.
- Choose a place for the second jar that allows you to shake the jar often until the candy dissolves.

Results Shaking the jar dissolves more of the candy.

Why? Both candy pieces are soluble in the water. Vigorous movement causes the water to rub against the candy, knocking off small pieces that **dissolve**. Similarly, a mud ball in a fast-moving stream would dissolve quickly because it would have pieces knocked off by the moving water. Hard mud balls in a pond would dissolve slowly, as did the candy in the undisturbed jar.

138. Rock Bridge

Purpose To demonstrate how natural bridges stand.

Materials 2 flat chairs the same height
books

Procedure
- Move the chairs about 12 inches (30 cm) apart.
- Lay one book on each chair with the edge of the books even with the edges of the chairs.
- Stack books on top of each other so that each book extends farther over the edge than the one below it.
- Continue stacking the books until one book overlaps the stack from both chairs to form a bridge.

Results No part of the bottom books overlaps the edge of the chair. Each book above the bottom book extends over the chair's edge until the top book is completely past the edges of the chairs.

Why? All objects behave as if their weight is located in one spot called the **center of gravity**. The book bridge is supported because the center of gravity of each side of the bridge is over a chair. In nature, natural rock bridges are formed by **weathering** and erosional processes. These bridges balance because the particles making up the bridge overlap in such a way that they place the center of gravity of the structure over the supporting sides.

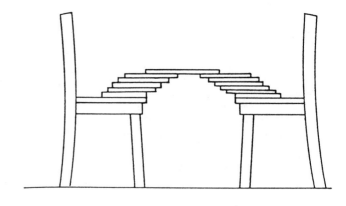

139. Tip

Purpose To determine if air has weight.

Materials modeling clay
yardstick (meterstick)
9-inch (23-cm) balloon
string
masking tape
2-foot (60-cm) thick cord
straight pen

Procedure

■ Place a piece of clay on one end of the yardstick (meterstick).

■ Inflate the balloon to its maximum size and use string to attach it to the yardstick on the end opposite the clay.

■ Place a small strip of tape about 1 inch (2.5 cm) long on the side of the inflated balloon, near the neck.

■ Use the thick cord to suspend the yardstick. Move the cord so that the stick balances.

■ Attach the top end of the cord to the side of a table or door frame so that the yardstick hangs freely.

■ Slowly insert the pin through the strip of tape and into the balloon. Remove the pin.

Results The end of the stick with the clay tips downward as the air leaves the balloon.

Why? Air has **weight**. As the air leaves the balloon, the side of the stick with the balloon becomes lighter. The Earth is surrounded by an ocean of air, which weighs so much that every square inch of the Earth supports about 14.7 pounds of air (1 square centimeter supports 1 kg of air).

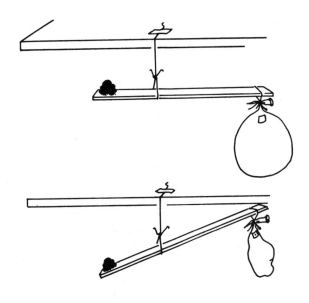

140. Push Up

Purpose To demonstrate the strength of atmospheric pressure.

Materials bowl large enough to hold a glass on its side
tap water
drinking glass

Procedure

■ Fill the bowl ¾ full with water.

■ Turn the glass on its side and push it beneath the surface of the water. The glass should fill with water.

■ Keep the glass under the water and turn it so that its mouth points down.

■ Slowly lift the glass leaving about 1 inch (1.25 cm) of the mouth under the water's surface.

Results The water remains inside the glass.

Why? The air pushing down on the surface of the water outside the glass extends upward hundreds of miles (km). The pressure of this air is called **atmospheric pressure**. This pressure is great enough to support the **weight** of the water inside the glass.

Thus, the water level inside the glass remains higher than the water level in the bowl.

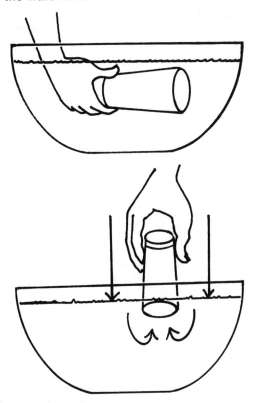

141. Increasing

Purpose To determine how temperature affects air pressure.

Materials   empty glass soft-drink bottle
9-inch (23-cm) balloon

Procedure
- Place the open bottle in the freezer for 1 hour.
- Remove the bottle from the freezer.
- Stretch the opening of the balloon over the mouth of the bottle.
- Allow the bottle to stand at room temperature for 15 minutes.

Results The balloon partially inflates.

Why? The air inside the bottle **contracts** when cooled. This allows more air to enter the bottle. The balloon seals the bottle; as the air inside heats, it expands and moves into the balloon, causing it to inflate. Air in the **atmosphere** contracts and expands as it is cooled and heated as did the air in the bottle. Expanding warm air rises and decreases atmospheric pressure; the pressure increases as the air cools and descends. Temperature is just one factor that affects

atmospheric pressure, but a rise in pressure is a good indication that nice weather can be expected.

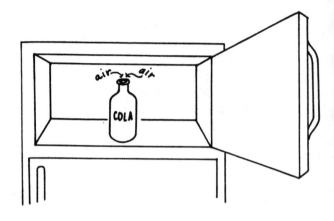

---

142. Up Draft

Purpose To determine the effect that temperature has on air movement.

Materials   scissors   cellophane tape
ruler   desk lamp
tissue paper   adult helper
thread

Procedure
- Cut a 2-inch (6-cm) diameter spiral from the tissue paper.
- Cut a piece of thread 6 inches (15 cm) long.
- Tape one end of the piece of thread to the center of the paper spiral.
- Turn the desk lamp so that the light points upward.
- Ask an adult to hold the end of the thread, and position the paper spiral about 4 inches (10 cm) above the light.
CAUTION: *Do not allow the paper to touch the light bulb.*

Results The paper spiral twirls.

Why? The energy from the light heats the air above it. The air molecules move faster and farther apart as

they absorb energy. The separation of the molecules makes the air lighter and it rises upward. Cooler air rushes in to take the place of the warmer rising air. As long as the lamp is on, warm air rises and cooler air moves in to take its place producing air movements called **convection currents** (movement of air due to differences in temperature).

143. Speedy

Purpose To demonstrate how wind speed is measured.

Materials masking tape
pencil
protractor
12-inch (30-cm) piece of sewing thread
ping pong ball
helper

Procedure

■ Tape the pencil to the straight edge of the protractor as shown in the diagram.

■ Tape one end of the thread to the ping pong ball.

■ Tape the other end of the thread to the center of the straight edge of the protractor. The thread should hang so that it crosses the 90 degree mark on the protractor.

■ Use the pencil as a handle and hold the instrument so that the ball is about 12 inches (30 cm) from your helper's face.

■ Ask your helper to gently blow a stream of air toward the ball on the instrument.

■ Observe where the string crosses the protractor.

■ Ask your helper to blow harder as you observe the position of the string on the protractor, again.

Results With a gentle breath, the string moves a few degrees. But blowing harder causes the string to move a greater number of degrees.

Why? The instrument you built is called an anemometer. An **anemometer** is an instrument that tells how fast the wind blows. Moving air hits the ping pong ball causing it to move. The speed of the wind hitting the ball is determined by the number of degrees the ball moves, which is indicated by the position of the string across the protractor.

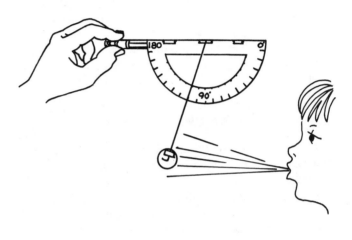

144. Which Way?

Purpose To determine why the air is cooler in the winter.

Materials flashlight
1 sheet of dark paper

Procedure

■ In a dark room, hold the flashlight about 6 inches (15 cm) directly above the dark paper.

■ Observe the size and shape of the light pattern formed.

■ Tilt the flashlight and observe the light pattern again.

Results The light coming straight down produces a small, bright circle. Slanting the flashlight produces a larger, less bright pattern on the paper.

Why? In the winter, the Sun does not heat the Earth as much as it does during other times of the year. The position of the Sun in the sky during the winter is not as high in the sky as during other seasons. Winter sunlight comes in at an angle, like the light from the slanted flashlight. This light travels through more of the **atmosphere** and covers a large area on the surface where it strikes. These slanted rays are spread over a larger area and do not heat as much as when the rays shine straight down.

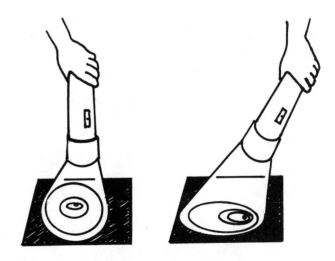

145. Wet Bulb

Purpose To determine how a psychrometer measures relative humidity.

Materials two thermometers
1 cotton ball
tap water
fan

Procedure
- Place both thermometers on a table.
- Record the temperature on both thermometers.
- Wet the cotton ball with water and place it over the bulb of one of the thermometers.
- Place the fan so that it blows across both bulbs.
- Record the temperature of the two bulbs after 5 minutes.

Results The thermometer that has its bulb covered with wet cotton has a lower temperature.

Why? The wet-bulb thermometer is cooled as the water **evaporates** from the cotton. The faster the water evaporates, the lower the temperature on this thermometer. The dry bulb thermometer records the air temperature. Low **relative humidity** (amount of water vapor in the air compared with the amount that the air

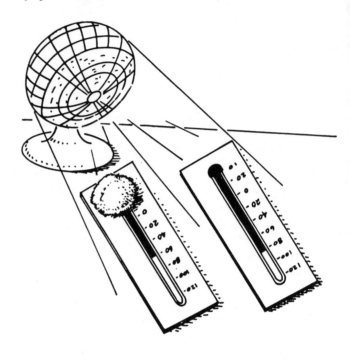

can hold at that temperature) is indicated by a large difference between the wet and dry bulb reading. The instrument that measures relative humidity is called a **psychrometer**.

146. Soggy

Purpose To demonstrate how salt is used to measure humidity.

Materials scissors
black construction paper
2 saucers
teaspoon (5 ml)
table salt
pencil

Procedure
- Cut a piece of black construction paper to fit in the bottom of both saucers.
- Sprinkle ½ teaspoon (2.5 ml) of salt on the black paper in each saucer.
- Hold your mouth about 6 inches (15 cm) from one of the saucers.
- Exhale toward the salt in one saucer for about 2 minutes.
- Use the pencil to stir the salt in both saucers.

Results The salt that was breathed on forms clumps when stirred, while the salt crystals in the other dish remain separate.

Why? Exhaled breath contains water vapor. Table salt has a strong attraction for water and readily absorbs moisture from the air or your breath. The water causes the salt crystals to stick together. Air that contains a large amount of water causes salt to become soggy. You can tell the humidity is high when salt is difficult to shake from saltshakers.

147. Dew Point

Purpose To determine the temperature at which dew forms.

Materials drinking glass
           ice
           tap water
           thermometer

Procedure
- Fill the glass with ice.
- Add enough water to cover the ice.
- Place the thermometer in the glass of icy water.
- Watch the outside of the glass and record the temperature when water is observed on the outside of the glass.
- Perform this experiment several times, selecting days that have different humidities.

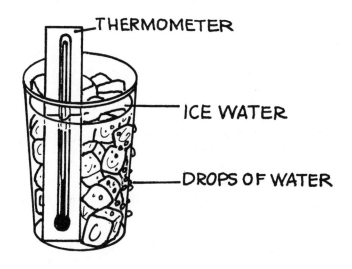

Results When the humidity is high, the water collects on the glass at a higher temperature.

Why? Water vapor in the air **condenses** (changes to a liquid) when it touches the cool surface of the glass. The **dew point** is the temperature at which water vapor condenses. A high dew point indicates a high **humidity** (amount of water in the air).

148. Cooling

Purpose To determine how color effects the dew point.

Materials 1 sheet white construction paper
           1 sheet black construction paper

Procedure
- Perform this experiment on several different calm, clear nights and during different seasons of the year.
- Just before sunset, place both sheets on paper on the ground, out in the open.
- Check the papers every half hour for 2 hours.

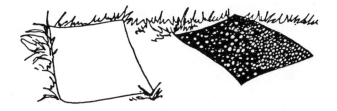

Results Dew forms first on the black paper; on some nights, dew is found *only* on the black paper.

Why? **Dew** (moisture condensed from the air) forms on an object when that object cools enough to cause water vapor in the air to **condense**. Dark materials **radiate** or lose heat energy faster than do materials with a light color, so the **dew point** is reached faster by the black paper. On some nights, the papers do not get cold enough for the dew to form at all. The best results occur when the days are warm and humid and the nights are cool, calm, and clear.

149. Frosty

Purpose To determine how frost forms.

Materials drinking glass

Procedure
- Place a drinking glass in the freezer for 30 minutes.
- Remove the glass and allow it to stand undisturbed for 30 seconds.
- Scratch the cloudy formation on the outside of the glass with your fingernail.
- Perform this experiment several times, selecting days with differing humidities.

Results The glass looks frosty, and a very thin layer of soft ice seems to be stuck to the outside of the glass.

Why? Frost forms when water vapor changes directly to a solid—ice. The glass is cold enough to cause the water vapor in the air to cool so quickly that it **sublimes** (changes from a gas to a solid without forming a liquid).

150. Drops

Purpose To determine how raindrops form.

Materials tap water
quart (liter) jar with lid
ice cubes

Procedure
- Pour enough water into the jar to cover the bottom.
- Turn the jar lid upside down and set it over the mouth of the jar.
- Put 3 or 4 ice cubes inside the lid.
- Observe the underside of the lid for 10 minutes.

Results The lid looks wet, and finally water drops form on the underside of the lid.

Why? Some of the water in the bottom of the jar **evaporates** (changes into a gas). The water vapor **condenses** and then changes back to a liquid when it hits the cool underside of the lid. As the amount of liquid increases, drops form on the underside of the lid. In nature, liquid water evaporates from open water areas such as streams, lakes, and oceans. This vapor rises and condenses as it hits the cooler upper air. **Clouds** are made of tiny drops of water suspended in the air. The tiny water drops join together, forming larger, heavier drops. The drops start falling when air can no longer support them. Raindrops usually have a diameter larger than 0.02 inches (0.05 cm). Some widely separated drops are smaller.

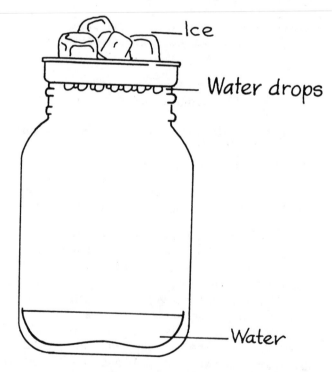

151. Bigger

Purpose To determine how tiny water droplets in clouds grow into raindrops.

Materials eyedropper
tap water
clear plastic lid (coffee can lid)
pencil

Procedure
- Fill the eyedropper with water.
- Hold the plastic lid in your hand, bottom side up.
- Squeeze as many separate drops of water as will fit on the lid.
- Quickly turn the lid over.
- Use the point of a pencil to move the tiny drops of water together.

Results Some of the water falls when the lid is inverted, leaving small drops on the lid. The small drops combine, forming larger drops that eventually fall.

Why? Water molecules have an attraction for each other. This attraction is due to the fact that each molecule has a positive and a negative side. The positive side of the molecule attracts the negative side of another molecule. The tiny water droplets on the plastic lid, as well as in **clouds**, join to form larger, heavier drops, which fall. The falling drops from clouds are called raindrops.

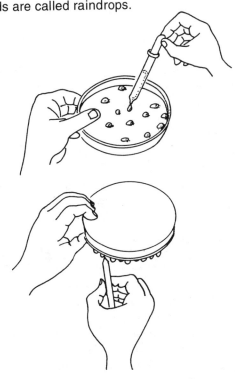

152. Rising Drops

Purpose To demonstrate how the speed and direction of air affect falling rain.

Materials plastic beach ball
fan

Procedure
- Inflate the ball.
- Turn the fan upward and switch to high speed.
- Place the ball over the blowing fan.
- Turn the speed of the fan to low speed.
- Observe the movement of the ball.

Results The ball floats above the fan when the fan is on high speed, but falls when the speed of the fan is decreased.

Why? The air above the fan, when it is on high, moves upward very quickly and has enough force to lift the ball. The pull of **gravity** prevents the ball from rising very high. In a thunderstorm, some raindrops do not fall to the ground when the speed of the updraft is high. The force of the air moving upward at a high speed tears apart large raindrops that are heavy enough to fall, and the tiny droplets remain suspended in the air.

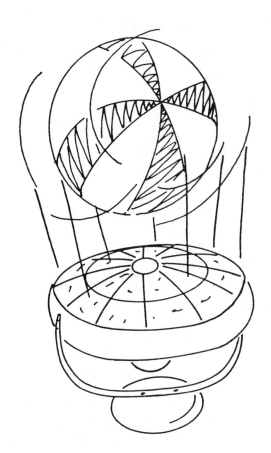

153. Floating Flakes

Purpose To demonstrate why snowflakes float.

Materials 2 sheets of notebook paper

Procedure
- Crumple one of the paper sheets into a ball.
- Hold the flat sheet in one hand and the crumpled sheet in your other hand.
- Drop both sheets at the same time.
- Observe which sheet of paper strikes the floor first.

Results The crumpled sheet hits the floor first; the flat sheet floats slowly downward.

Why? The downward pull of **gravity** is the same on both sheets of paper, but the upward force of air on each sheet is not the same. Raindrops and snowflakes are both made of water, but they have different shapes. The raindrop, like the crumpled paper, takes up a small amount of space and falls more quickly than does the flat sheet of paper, which behaves like a snowflake. The flat paper, like snowflakes, falls slowly because it has a greater exposed area and thus receives more upward force from the air.

154. Low Pressure

Purpose To demonstrate the formation and effect of low pressure.

Materials 2 9-inch (23-cm) balloons
ruler
sewing thread
cellophane tape
pencil

Procedure
- Inflate each balloon to the size of an apple and tie a knot.
- Attach a 12-inch (30-cm) thread to the top of each balloon.
- Tape the ends of each thread to the pencil so that the balloons hang about 3 inches (7.5 cm) apart.
- Hold the pencil level with the balloons about 3 inches (7.5 cm) from your face.
- Direct your exhaled breath between the balloons.

Results The balloons move together.

Why? The fast-moving air between the balloons reduces the air pressure on the insides of the balloons, and the air pressure on the outside pushes the balloons together. The rapidly rising air in a tornado creates a very low pressure area. The tornado acts like a huge vacuum cleaner, sucking in air, dirt, trees and other materials. These materials are lifted upward and then dropped, generally at some distance from their origin.

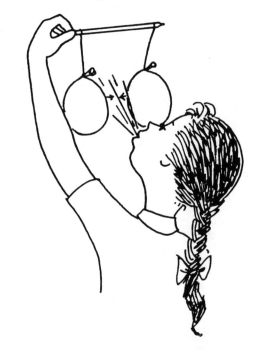

155. Divers

Purpose To determine how the buoyancy of ocean diving vessels changes.

Materials drinking glass
seltzer or club soda
raisins

Procedure
- Fill the drinking glass ¾ full with seltzer.
- Immediately add 5 raisins to the glass, one at a time.
- Wait and watch.

Results Bubbles collect on the raisins. The raisins rise to the surface, spin over, and fall to the bottom of the glass, where more bubbles start to stick to them again.

Why? The raisins sink when their **weight** is greater than the **buoyant force** (upward force that a liquid exerts on an object in it) exerted by the liquid. The gas bubbles act like tiny balloons that make the raisins light enough to float to the surface. When the bubbles are knocked off at the surface, the raisins sink to the bottom until more bubbles stick to them. Submersibles are ocean research vessels that allow oceanographers to work deep beneath the ocean's surface. The vessels rise and sink in the water, as do the raisins, by changing their buoyancy. The ocean research vessels rise by releasing liquids.

156. Bang!

Purpose To demonstrate how thunder is produced.

Materials paper lunch bag

Procedure
- Fill the bag by blowing into it.
- Twist the open end and hold it closed with your hand.
- Quickly and with force hit the bag with your free hand.

Results The bag breaks and a loud noise is heard.

Why? Hitting the bag causes the air inside to compress so quickly that the pressure breaks the bag. The air that rushes out pushes the air outside away from the bag. The air continues to move foreword in a wave. When the moving air reaches your ear, you hear a sound. Thunder is produced in a similar way. As lightning strikes, energy is given off that heats the air through which it passes. This heated air quickly expands, producing energetic waves of air resulting in a sound called thunder.

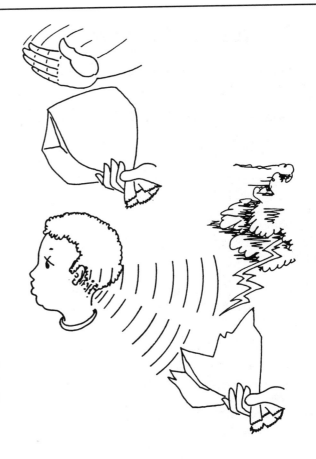

157. Curls

Purpose To determine if temperature affects the movement of water.

Materials pencil
5-ounce (150 ml) paper cup
1 quart (liter) small-mouth jar
masking tape
warm tap water
2 ice cubes
eyedropper
food coloring

Procedure

- Use the point of a pencil to punch four small holes near the bottom of the paper cup. The holes should be spaced evenly around the cup.
- Set the paper cup in the jar so that the rim rests on the mouth of the jar.
- Place a small piece of tape on the outside of the jar to mark a spot about ½ inch (1.25 cm) above the holes in the cup.
- Lift the cup and fill the jar to the top of the tape with warm tap water.
- Set the paper cup back in the jar and place the ice cubes in the cup.
- Wait 1 minute.

- Add three drops of food coloring to the water in the paper cup (avoid the ice cubes).

Results Colored water leaves the cup, twisting and curling as it flows downward through the warm water.

Why? The warm water enters the cup and is cooled by the ice cubes. The cold water in the cup **contracts** (moves closer together) and the warm water in the jar **expands** (moves farther apart). The contraction of the cold water makes it more dense than the warm water. The denser cold colored water sinks through the less dense warm water. The movement of water due to differences in temperature are called **convection currents**.

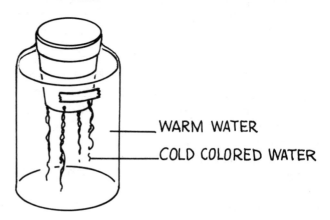

WARM WATER

COLD COLORED WATER

158. Wave Action

Purpose To demonstrate how wind produces water waves out at sea.

Materials large, shallow pan
tap water
drinking straw

Procedure

- Fill the pan ½ full with water.
- Hold one end of the straw close to the surface of the water.
- Blow air across the water's surface.
- Blow gently, then harder.

Results Waves formed on top of the water. The height of the waves varied with the change in strength of air flow.

Why? The energy from the moving air is transferred to the surface of the water. The height of the waves depends on the speed of the wind. The energized water is pushed upward, forming a wave. As the energy passes through the water, ripples of waves move out from the end of the straw.

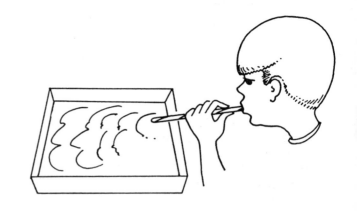

159. Up and Down

Purpose To demonstrate the motion of water waves.

Materials 6-foot (2-m) rope or strong cord

Procedure
- Tie one end of the rope to a door knob.
- Hold the other end of the rope in your hand and stretch the rope between you and the door.
- Gently move the rope up and down several times.

Results Waves move down the rope toward the door knob, but the rope does not move forward.

Why? Waves that move up and down like those along the rope or on the surface of water are called **transverse waves**. The top part of the wave is called the **crest**, and the bottom part is called the **trough**. The wave moves from one end of the rope to the other just as water waves move outward when you drop a rock into a pond. The water molecules in the pond, like the material in the rope, do not move forward. Only the energy of each wave moves forward.

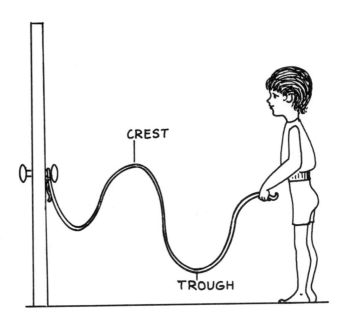

160. Mixer

Purpose To demonstrate how bottom sediment in lakes is mixed with water at upper levels.

Materials scissors
2-liter clear plastic soda bottle
tap water
4 tablespoons (60 ml) flour
quart (liter) jar
ice
blue food coloring
spoon
adult helper

Procedure
- Ask an adult helper to cut the top from the soda bottle.
- Fill the plastic bottle ½ full with water.
- Pour in the flour. Do not stir.
- Allow the plastic bottle to stand overnight so the flour can settle to the bottom.
- Fill the jar with ice, then add water to fill the jar. Allow it to stand for 5 minutes.
- Use the spoon to remove any undissolved ice cubes.
- Add enough food coloring to the cold water to produce a dark blue liquid.
- Ask your helper to tilt the plastic bottle slightly while you pour the cold colored water against the inside of the bottle.

Results The colored water sinks to the bottom of the bottle, causing the flour to be pushed upward on the opposite side.

Why? Cold water **contracts** (gets closer together) which makes the cold water denser than the warmer water in the bottle. The denser cold water sinks to the bottom of the bottle and pushes the sediment of flour upward where it mixes with the warmer water above. This is similar to the sinking of cold surface water in lakes. This descending water pushes the much needed food settled on the bottom of the lake up to the organisms living in the upper layers of the water.

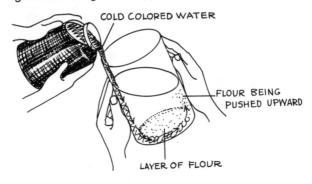

V
Physics

161. Spoon Bell

Purpose To determine what makes a sound loud or soft.

Materials metal spoon (thick, heavy spoons work best)
30 inches (75 cm) kite string

Procedure
- Tie the handle of the spoon at the mid point of the string.
- Wrap the ends of the string around your index fingers. Be sure that both strings are the same length.
- Place the tips of your index fingers in each ear.
- Lean over so that the spoon hangs freely and very gently tap the spoon against the side of a table.
- Repeat the previous step, but hit the spoon firmly against the table.

Results A soft sound like a bell is heard when the spoon is tapped gently on the table. A louder sound, much like a church bell, is heard when the spoon is struck firmly against the table.

Why? All sound is a form of wave motion that is produced when things **vibrate** (movement back and forth). Striking the spoon caused it to vibrate. The loudness or quietness of the sound produced by vibrating molecules depends on the **amplitude** (height) of the sound wave produced by the vibrating molecules. The higher the amplitude of the wave the louder the sound.

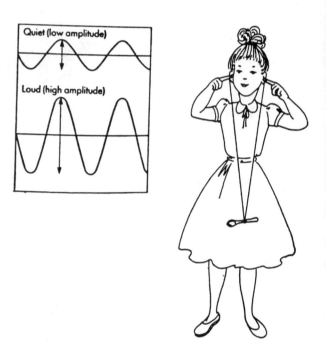

162. Humming Glass

Purpose To show how friction can cause a glass to vibrate.

Materials dishwashing liquid
tap water
sink or large pan
stemmed glassware (this will work better if the glass is very thin)
vinegar
small shallow bowl

Procedure
- Use the dishwashing liquid to make a warm, soapy water solution in a sink or large pan.
- Wash the glass and your hands in the warm, soapy water, and rinse well.
- Place the glass on a table.
- Pour a thin layer of vinegar into the small bowl.
- Hold the base of the glass against the table with one hand.
- Wet the index finger of your other hand with vinegar and gently rub your wet finger around the rim of the glass.

Results The glass starts to hum when its rim is rubbed.

Why? Washing the glass and your hands removes any oil that might act as a lubricant. The vinegar also **dissolves** any oil that might be present and increases the **friction** between your skin and the glass. Rubbing your finger around the rim causes the glass to **vibrate** because your finger skips and pulls at the glass. This causes the glass to vibrate. The pitch of the sound you hear is due to **frequency** (number of vibrations per second).

163. Twang

it to move up and down very quickly, producing a higher pitched sound.

Purpose To demonstrate the effect that length has on the sound of a vibrating material.

Materials ruler
table

Procedure
- Place the ruler on a table with about 10 inches (25 cm) of the ruler hanging over the edge of the table.
- Press the end of the ruler against the table with your hand.
- With your other hand, push the free end of the ruler down and then quickly release it.
- As the ruler moves, slide it quickly onto the table.
- Listen to the sounds produced.

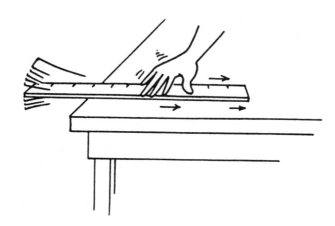

Results The sound produced changes from a low pitch to a high pitch as the length of the ruler extending over the edge of the table decreases.

Why? Sound is produced by vibrating materials. The **pitch** of the sound becomes higher as the number of **vibrations** increases. The longer the vibrating material, the slower the up-and-down movement and the lower the sound produced. Shortening the ruler causes

164. Bottle Organ

Purpose To demonstrate how frequency affects the pitch of sound.

Materials tap water
6 small-mouth bottles of comparable size
metal spoon

Procedure
- Pour different amounts of water in each bottle.
- Gently tap each bottle with the metal spoon.
- Note the difference in the pitch produced.

Results The bottle with the most water has the lowest pitch.

Why? Sounds are made by vibrating objects. The number of times the object **vibrates**—moves back and forth—is called the **frequency** of the sound. As the frequency increases, the **pitch** of the sound gets higher. Tapping on the bottle causes the bottle and its contents to vibrate. As the height of the water column increases, the pitch of the sound gets lower.

165. Cold Foot

Purpose To identify a good conductor of heat energy.

Materials aluminum foil
small throw rug or rug sample

Procedure
- Cut a piece of foil that is a little bigger than your foot.
- Place the foil and the rug on a tile floor. Allow them to remain undisturbed for 10 minutes.
- Put one bare foot on the aluminum foil and the other on the rug.
- Observe any difference between the feel of the temperature of the aluminum foil and that of the rug.

Results The metal foil feels colder than the carpet.

Why? Things feel cold to the touch when heat energy is drawn away from your skin; things feel warm when heat energy is transferred to your skin. A heat **conductor** is a material that allows heat to move through it. The aluminum feels colder than the carpet because it is a good heat conductor and the heat leaves your foot and moves through the metal. The carpet is a poor heat conductor and actually blocks heat loss from your foot.

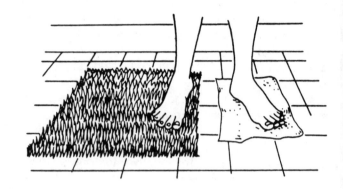

166. Expando

Purpose To demonstrate how pressure affects the volume of a marshmallow.

Materials black marker
1 miniature marshmallow
small, transparent, glass bottle with a
    mouth slightly larger than the
    marshmallow (such as a salt shaker)
modeling clay
drinking straw
mirror

Procedure
- Use the marker to draw a face on one end of the marshmallow.
- Place the marshmallow inside the bottle.
- Wrap the clay around the straw about 1 inch (2.5 cm) from its end.
- Place the short end of the straw into the bottle.
- Seal the mouth of the bottle with the clay.
- Stand in front of a mirror and turn the bottle so that the face on the marshmallow faces the mirror.
- Look at the mirror image of the marshmallow while you suck the air out of the bottle through the straw. This should be difficult if there are no leaks.
- Continue to look at the marshmallow's mirror image and remove the straw from your mouth.

Results The face on the marshmallow expands when you suck on the straw then return to its original size when you take the straw out of your mouth.

Why? The marshmallow is a spongy solid with air trapped inside the spaces. Sucking air out of the bottle decreases the pressure inside the bottle causing the air inside the marshmallow to expand. Removing the straw from your mouth allows air to rush into the bottle increasing the pressure and causing the marshmallow to return to its original size.

167. Straight

Purpose To demonstrate that light travels in a straight line.

Materials scissors   modeling clay
ruler   flashlight
cardboard   index card

Procedure

- Cut three 6-inch (15-cm) squares from the cardboard.
- Cut 1-inch (2.5-cm) square notches from the center of one edge of each of the three cardboard squares.
- Use the clay to position the square about 4 inches (10 cm) apart with the notches aligned in a straight line.
- Lay the flashlight behind the column of cards.
- Use clay to position the index card like a screen at the other end of the column.
- Darken the room and observe any light pattern on the paper screen.
- Move the cardboard so that the notches are not in a straight line.
- Observe any light pattern on the paper screen.

Results Light appears on the screen only when the notches are in a straight line with each other.

Why? Light travels in a straight line. When the notches were in line, the light rays were able to pass through the openings, but when the notches were out of line, the rays were blocked by the cardboard.

168. See Through

Purpose To test the movement of light through different materials.

Materials cardboard
wax paper
plastic sandwich bag

Procedure

- One by one, hold the plastic, wax paper, and cardboard pieces in front of your eyes while you note any differences in how objects in the room appear.

Results There is little or no change in appearance when things are observed through the plastic. The wax paper makes objects look dull and frosty, while nothing can be seen through the cardboard.

Why? In order for you to see anything, light must be reflected from the object you are looking at to your eyes. The clear plastic is an example of a **transparent** material. Transparent means that light rays move straight through the material and allows you to see objects as they are. **Translucent** materials, like wax paper, change the direction of the light rays that pass through. This change in direction makes objects look dull, frosty, and sometimes distorted. Cardboard is an opaque material—no light rays can pass through. Without light rays passing through to your eye, nothing on the opposite side of opaque materials can be seen.

169. Rosy Skin

Purpose   To determine how filters affect light.

Materials   flashlight

Procedure
NOTE: *This experiment takes place in a darkened room.*

- Hold the flashlight under your hand.
- Move the light around behind your fingers and palm.
- Observe any light that passes through.

Results   Parts of your hand appear rosy in color.

Why?   Your flesh and skin act like filters. A filter is any material that **absorbs** some of the colors in light and allows others to pass through. Red filters absorb all colors except red which passes through. Your skin takes on a rosy color because the red blood under the skin acts like a red filter—red light passes through and other colors are stopped.

170. Waves

Purpose   To demonstrate how light waves travel.

Materials   Slinky®, about 4-inches (10-cm) long
helper

Procedure
- Have your helper hold one end of the Slinky and stretch it to about four times its length while you hold the other end.
- Shake your end of the Slinky up and down several times.
- Notice how the Slinky moves.

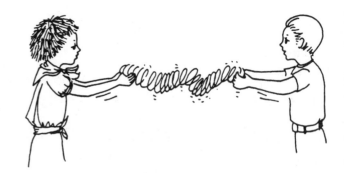

Results   Shaking the Slinky up and down makes it look like water waves.

Why?   The up-and-down movement of the Slinky represents a **transverse wave**. These are like water waves in that they have high and low parts called **crests** and **troughs**. Light also travels in transverse waves, but can travel through space.

171. Pepper Run

Purpose To make black pepper run across a bowl of water when soap is added.

Materials   black pepper
2-quart (2-liter) bowl full of tap water
liquid detergent
saucer
toothpicks

Procedure
- Sprinkle the pepper over the surface of the water in the bowl.
- Pour a few drops of liquid detergent into the saucer and dip the end of the toothpick into it.
- Insert the wet end of the toothpick in the center of the pepper.

NOTE: *All the soap must be washed out of the bowl and fresh water used before the experiment can be repeated.*

Results The pepper breaks in the center and runs toward the sides of the bowl.

Why? Each pepper speck is part of a tug-of-war battle. Before adding the soap, the surface water mole-cules surrounding the pepper specks pulled on them with equal force in all directions. Placing the soap in the center weakened the pull of the water molecules in that area. The stronger pulling water molecules without soap on the opposite side of the pepper specks pulled them toward the side of the bowl.

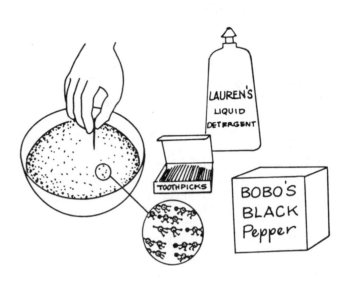

172. Air Car

Purpose To demonstrate how friction effects motion.

Materials   scissors   notebook paper
ruler   9-inch (23-cm) balloon
cardboard   pencil
empty thread   adult helper
  spool
glue

Procedure
- Cut a 4-inch (10-cm) square from the cardboard.
- Ask an adult to punch a hole equal in size to the hole in the thread spool through the center of the cardboard square.
- Glue the empty thread spool over the hole in the cardboard. Be sure the hole in the spool lines up with the hole in the cardboard.
- Place a bead of glue around the base of the spool.
- Cut and glue a circle of paper over the top end of the thread spool. Allow the glue to dry for several hours.
- Use a pencil to punch a hole in the paper circle to line up with the hole in the spool.
- Inflate the balloon and twist the end.
- Stretch the mouth of the balloon over the top of the spool.
- Untwist the balloon and give the cardboard a little push. Observe its motion.

Results As the balloon deflates, the cardboard skims across the table.

Why? The air flowing from the balloon through the holes forms a thin layer of air between the cardboard and table. This air layer reduces **friction** (a force that tries to stop movement), allowing the cardboard to move quickly across the table.

GLUE
SEAL

173. Roller

Purpose To determine how different surfaces affect friction.

Materials 2 books
24-inch (60-cm) string
rubber band
ruler
10 round marking pens

Procedure

- Stack the books on a table.
- Tie the string around the bottom book.
- Attach the string to the rubber band.
- Move the stack of books by pulling on the rubber band.
- Measure how far the rubber band stretches.
- Place the 10 marking pens under the stack of books.
- Move the books by pulling on the rubber band.
- Observe how far the rubber band stretches.

Results The rubber band stretches more when the bottom book sits flat against the table than when it is placed on the pens.

Why? The flat surface of the book slides across the table and the round pens roll across the table.

Things that roll cause less friction than things that slide. Thus, there is less friction between the pens and the table than between the book and the table.

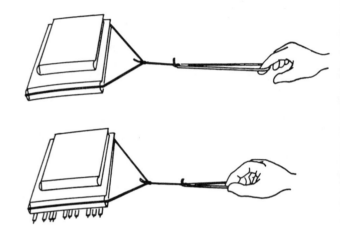

174. Energy Change

Purpose To demonstrate the effect that height has on the energy of a moving object.

Materials scissors
8-ounce (236 ml) paper cup
ruler with a center groove
pencil
marble
book

Procedure

- Cut a 1½-inch (3.75-cm) square section from the top of the paper cup.
- Place the cup over the ruler. The end of the ruler should touch the back edge of the cup.
- Raise the opposite end of the ruler and rest it on the pencil.
- Place the marble in the center groove of the ruler at the ruler's highest end.
- Release the marble and observe the cup.
- Raise the end of the ruler and rest it on the edge of the book.
- Again, position the marble in the groove at the ruler's highest end.
- Release the marble and observe the cup.

Results The cup moves when the marble strikes it. The cup moved further when the ruler rested on the book.

Why? Objects at rest have **potential energy**. The higher the object sits above the ground, the greater is its potential energy. When objects fall or roll down an incline, their potential energy changes into **kinetic energy**—energy of motion. Increasing the height from which the marble rolled gave it more energy, causing it to strike the cup with more force. Therefore, the cup moved further.

175. Wind Brake

Purpose To demonstrate the effect of air on motion.

Materials empty, styrofoam thread spool
scissors
ruler
stiff paper (an index card will work)
string
cellophane tape
2 paper clips
knitting needle
adult helper

Procedure

■ Ask an adult helper to cut four slits at right angles in the thread spool.
■ Cut four 3-inch × 1½-inch (7.5-cm × 4-cm) cards from the stiff paper.
■ Cut a 16-inch (40-cm) piece of string and tape it to the side of the spool.
■ Attach two paper clips to the end of the string.
■ Put the knitting needle through the center of the spool.
■ Wind the string around the spool.
■ Hold the knitting needle and observe the speed of the unwinding string.

■ Insert the four paper cards in the slits in the spool.
■ Wind the string around the spool.
■ Hold the knitting needle and observe the speed of the unwinding string.

Results The spool turns more slowly when the paper cards are in place.

Why? Gravity causes the paper clips to fall and pull the attached string with them. As the string unwinds, it spins the spool. Air pushes against the paper cards as the spool spins, reducing the speed of the turning spool.

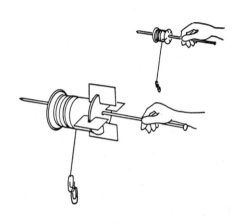

176. Bonk!

Purpose To determine how energy can change its form.

Materials scissors
ruler
string
book
duct tape
2 small rubber balls of equal size

Procedure

■ Cut a 24-inch (60-cm) piece of string.
■ Insert one end of the ruler into a book.
■ Lay the book on the edge of a table so the ruler sticks over the edge of the table.
■ Tie the center of the string around the end of the ruler.
■ Use very small pieces of tape to attach the hanging ends of the string to the balls. The tape sticks best if the balls are clean and oil-free.
■ The strings on the balls must be the same length.
■ Pull the balls away from each other and release them.

Results The balls continue to hit and bounce away from each other until they finally stop moving.

Why? Energy is never lost or created, only changed to another form. **Kinetic energy** in moving things that accomplishes work, in this case moves the balls, is called is **mechanical energy**. When the balls collide, part of the mechanical energy from the balls is changed into heat and sound energy. When all of the mechanical energy has been changed, the balls stop.

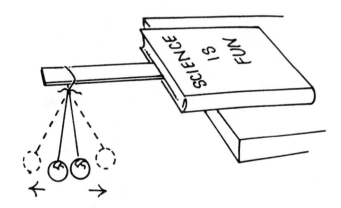

177. Snap!

Purpose To demonstrate that an object remains stationary due to inertia.

Materials scissors
ruler
typing paper
unopened can of soda

Procedure

- Cut a 4-inch × 10-inch (10-cm × 25-cm) strip of paper.
- Lay the paper strip on a clean, dry table.
- Place the soda can over one end of the paper. NOTE: *Be sure that the bottom of the can is clean and dry.*
- Hold the other end of the paper and push it close to the can.
- Quickly snap the paper away from the can in a straight line.

Results If you pulled the paper quickly enough, it moved from under the can, but the can remained upright and in the same place.

Why? **Inertia** is a resistance to any change in motion. An object that is stationary remains that way until some force causes it to move. The can is not attached to the paper. Because of the can's inertia, it remains stationary even though the paper moves forward.

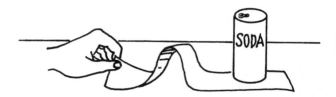

178. Plop!

Purpose To demonstrate that an object continues to move due to inertia.

Materials 5 books
chair or cart with rollers

Procedure

- Stack the books on the edge of the chair seat.
- Push the chair forward then quickly stop the chair.

Results The books move forward and fall to the floor.

Why? **Inertia** is a resistance to any change in motion. A moving object remains in motion until some force stops it. The books are moving at the same speed as the chair. They are not attached to the chair. Therefore, when the chair stops, the books continue to move forward. They would continue to move forward in the air until hitting some other object except that the force of **gravity** pulls them down. Air molecules also hit the books, slowing their forward motion.

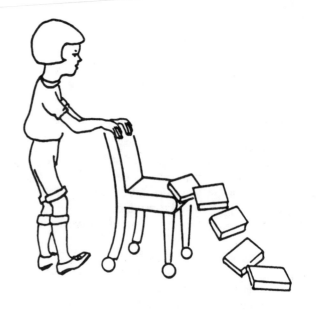

179. Crash!

Purpose To demonstrate that moving objects have inertia.

Materials 1 ruler
1 book, about 1 inch (2.5 cm) thick
masking tape
pencil
piece of modeling clay, size of a walnut
small toy car that can roll on the ruler

Procedure

- Raise one end of the ruler and place it on the edge of the book.
- Tape the other end of the ruler to a table.
- Tape the pencil perpendicular to, and about 2 toy car lengths from the end of the ruler.
- Make a clay figure similar to a snowman.
- Flatten the bottom of the clay figure and gently rest it on the hood of the toy car. You want the clay figure to fall off the car easily, so do not press the clay against the car.
- Position the car with its clay figure at the top of the raised ruler.
- Release the car and allow it to roll down the ruler and collide into the pencil.

Results The car with the clay figure moves down the ruler. The car stops when it hits the pencil, but the clay figure continues to move forward for a distance.

Why? The car and clay figure both have **inertia**, a resistance to a change in motion. Once started, both continue to move until some outside force acts against them, causing them to stop. When the pencil stopped the car's motion, the clay figure continued to move forward. The air molecules slowed the clay figure's forward motion as **gravity** pulled the clay figure down.

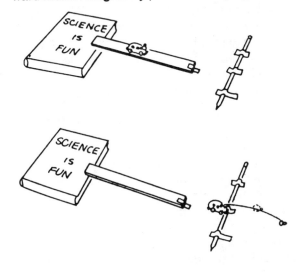

180. Spool Racer

Purpose To demonstrate the transformation of energy.

Materials rubber band (slightly longer than a thread spool)
empty thread spool
2 round toothpicks
masking tape
metal washer (diameter must be smaller than that of the spool)

Procedure

- Insert the rubber band through the hole in the spool.
- Put one toothpick through the loop formed by the rubber band at one end of the spool.
- Center the toothpick on the end of the spool, and secure the toothpick to the spool with tape.
- At the other end of the spool, thread the rubber band through the hole in the washer.
- Put the second toothpick through the loop in the rubber band. Do not attach it to the spool.
- Hold the spool steady with one hand, and with the index finger of your other hand turn the unattached toothpick around and around in a clockwise direction to wind the rubber band tightly.

- Place the spool on a flat, smooth surface such as the floor, and let go.
- Observe the movement of the spool, rubber band, and toothpicks.

Results As the rubber band unwinds, the spool turns, turning the toothpick taped to the spool. The spool moves forward.

Why? There are two basic forms of energy: **kinetic** (energy of motion), and **potential** (stored energy). It took energy stored in the muscles of your body to wind the rubber band. As long as you prevented the rubber band from turning, by holding the stick, the energy was stored (potential). Releasing the stick allowed the rubber band to unwind; thus, the stored energy in the twisted rubber band was transformed into a form of kinetic energy that accomplished work, called **mechanical energy**.

181. Spinner

Purpose To determine the effect of ball bearings on motion.

Materials   1-gallon paint can (4-liter) (one that has never been opened)
6 marbles
3 heavy books

Procedure

- Place the can on a table.
- Space the marbles evenly around the rim of the can.
- Balance a stack of books on top of the marbles.
- Use your hand to push gently against one corner of the stack of books.
- Observe the movement of the books.

Results The books spin around easily on top of the marbles.

Why? Wheels allow you to move things more easily, and ball bearings within wheels allow them to rotate faster. **Ball bearings** are spheres placed between a wheel and an axle. These balls reduce the **friction** (the resistance to motion) between the surface of the wheel and the axle. Without the ball bearings, the surfaces would rub together because even very slick

materials have slight bumps on their surfaces. As a wheel turns, the bumps on the surface of the wheel catch on the bumps of the axle's surface, thereby slowing the wheel's rotation. The marble bearings in this experiment rotate as the book pushes against them, and things that roll cause less friction than things that slide. Since the surface of the marbles roll over the book, there is less friction. The motion of the marbles and the reduction of friction between the book and the marbles increases the rotation speed of the book.

---

182. Toothy

Purpose To determine how gears change movement from one direction to another.

Materials   modeling clay
12 round toothpicks
2 pencils

Procedure

- Slightly flatten two walnut-size balls of clay to form two wheels.
- Stick 6 toothpicks into the sides of each clay wheel. Be sure the toothpicks are evenly spaced around the clay pieces.
- Form gear A by pushing a pencil through the center of one clay wheel.
- Hollow out the hole with the pencil so that the clay wheel easily turns around the pencil.
- Form gear B by inserting a pencil through the center of the second clay wheel.
- Squeeze the clay around the pencil so that the clay piece and the pencil turn together.
- Place gear A on a table; hold the pencil vertically to keep the gear in place.
- Hold gear B in a vertical position with its toothpicks between the toothpicks of gear A, as indicated in the diagram. NOTE: *The pencil should be horizontal.*

- Rotate the pencil of gear B in a counterclockwise direction.
- Observe the direction of movement of gear A.

Results Gear B rotates vertically in a counterclockwise direction; the teeth of the two gears push against each other, causing gear A to rotate horizontally in a clockwise direction.

Why? **Gears** are wheels with teeth around the outer rim. When the teeth of two gears fit together and one gear turns, it will cause the other gear to turn. In this experiment, the toothpicks in the clay wheels act as gear teeth. When the gears are of equal size and have the same number of gear teeth, as in this experiment, they both turn at the same speed. Fitting the gears together at an angle changes the direction of rotation of the two gears.

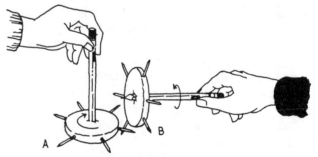

183. Wedge

Purpose To demonstrate how a wedge works.

Materials piece of cardboard
pencil

Procedure
- Lay the cardboard on a table.
- Press the pencil eraser down against the cardboard. Press hard.
- Observe what happens.
- Press the sharp point of the pencil against the cardboard, as hard as before.
CAUTION: *Be sure your hand is not under the cardboard.*
- Observe what happens.

Results The eraser presses the cardboard down, but the eraser does not stick into the cardboard. The sharp point of the pencil sticks into the cardboard.

Why? The pencil point acts like a **wedge** (any pie-shaped material used to lift, pry open, or split apart a material). The tapered, pointed end of the pencil acts as a **wedge** and sticks into the cardboard. The point of the pencil enters the paper first and makes a path

for the larger part of the pencil to follow. A wedge is a simple tool used to split logs.

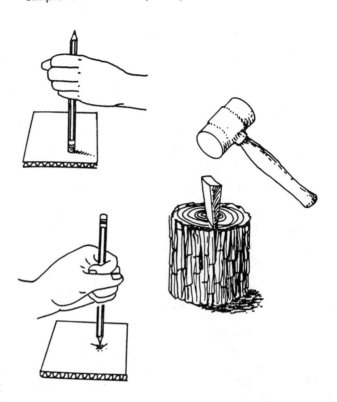

184. Lifter

Purpose To determine how a screw works.

Materials large screw

Procedure
- Hold the head of the screw with one hand.
- Put two fingernails on the first ridge at the tip of the screw.
- Turn the head of the screw clockwise.

Results As the screw turns, the ridges spiral downward. Your fingers stay in place and this unique winding road moves past them.

Why? The screw is an example of a simple machine called an **inclined plane** that is wrapped around a cylinder. The screw is like a winding **wedge**. The closer the threads are together, the easier it is to turn the screw. Screws are used to connect things, but they are also used to lift things; for example, screw jacks lift houses and cars.

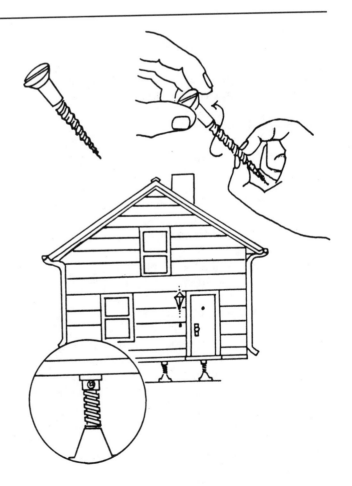

185. Ramp

Purpose To demonstrate that a winding mountain road is an inclined plane.

Materials scissors   pencil
ruler   cellophane tape
sheet of paper

Procedure
- Cut a 5-inch (13-cm) square from the paper.
- Draw a diagonal line across the square and cut across the line.
- Color the longest edge of the paper triangle with the pencil.
- Tape the triangle to the pencil as shown in the diagram.
- Wind the paper onto the pencil.

Results The colored side of the triangle is shaped like a ramp. Wrapping the paper around the pencil makes it look like a winding road or a screw.

Why? An **inclined plane** is a sloped surface. Like the threads on a screw, a winding road is an inclined plane. If the road could be unwound, it would look like the long, colored side of the paper triangle. It is true that it is farther up a road winding around a mountain than it would be directly up the mountain's side, but it takes much less effort to travel the longer distance. The inclined plane is a simple machine that makes a job easier. In this case, the job is climbing a mountain.

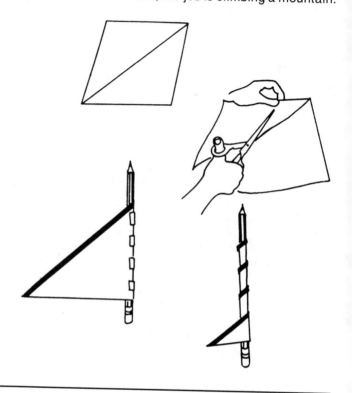

186. Upward

Purpose To determine why the shape of an airplane's wing is important for flight.

Materials scissors
ruler
typing paper

Procedure
- Cut a 2-inch × 10-inch (5-cm × 25-cm) strip from the paper.
- Hold one end of the paper against your chin, just below your bottom lip.
- Blow just above the top of the paper.
- Observe the movement of the paper strip.

Results The paper lifted upward.

Why? The shape of the top of an airplane's wing is more curved than the wing's bottom. Because of this design, air molecules move faster across the wing's top than across its bottom. **Bernoulli's principle** states that faster moving fluids, such as air, exert less pressure than slower moving fluids. Thus, the air over the top of the wing moves more quickly so the pressure on top of the wing is less than the pressure under the wing. This difference in pressure causes the wing to lift.

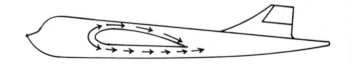

187. Super Straw

Purpose To determine how a straw works.

Materials drinking straw
bottle of soda

Procedure
- Place a straw in a bottle of soda.
- Suck on the straw with your mouth.
- Observe the results.

Results The soda moves up the straw and into your mouth.

Why? Gravity pulls the air molecules surrounding the straw down, putting pressure on the soda. When you suck the air out of the straw, the soda has room to move up into the empty straw.

The pressure of the air in the bottle is due to the total mass of air above the surface of the liquid. This mass rises for miles (km) above the liquid's surface, and its **weight** is great enough to hold up the straw full of soda.

188. Off Target

Purpose To determine the path of an object dropped from a moving body.

Materials 1 cup (250 ml) rice, uncooked
sock
pencil

Procedure
- Pour the rice into the sock.
- Tie a knot in the sock.
- Lay the pencil on the ground to mark the target position.
- Stand about 10 yards (10 m) from the target.
- Hold the sock in your hand to the side of your body about waist high.
- Run forward toward the target so that as you pass, the target will be to your side.
- Drop the sock at the moment the sock is above the target.
- Stop running as soon as the sock is released.
- Observe where the sock lands.

Results The sock lands on the ground past the target.

Why? Gravity starts pulling the sock down at the moment it is released, but the sock has the same forward horizontal speed as your running speed. It continues to move forward, slowing due to air resistance, and at the same time is pulled downward by gravity until it strikes the ground at a point past the target. All objects with a horizontal speed accompanied by a downward increase in speed due to gravity move forward in a curved path.

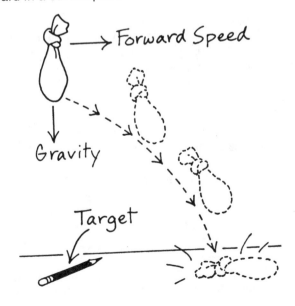

189. Shape Up

Purpose To determine how shape affects speed.

Materials   card table
2 books of equal thickness
2 jar lids, the same size
1 large roll of masking tape
marble
masking tape
helper

Procedure

- Tilt the card table by placing a book under two of the legs.
- Place the lid tops together and tape their edges to form a disk.
- Ask your helper to hold the disk made from the lids at the top of the incline while you hold the marble and roll of tape in line with the disk.
- Release all three objects at once.

Results The marble rolls fastest, with the lid disk coming in second, and the tape last.

Why? The rolling speed is related to the distribution of **weight** around the object's **center of gravity** (the point at which an object balances). The center of gravity of all the objects in this experiment is at their geometric center, but each has a different weight distribution. The closer the weight is to the center of gravity, the less energy it takes to rotate the weight. Given the same amount of energy, the marble moved fastest because its weight is closest to its center of gravity and the hollow tape roll moved the slowest because it's weight is located farthest from its center of gravity.

190. Breakthrough

Purpose To demonstrate how the shape of an object affects its falling speed.

Materials   2 sheets of typing paper   ruler
pencil   scissors
compass   cellophane tape

Procedure

- On each sheet of paper, draw a circle with an 8-inch (20-cm) diameter and cut both circles out.
- On one of the paper circles, cut a slit from the outside to the center.
- Overlap the cut edges to form a cone. Use a 1-inch (2.5-cm) piece of tape to secure the edges.
- Put an equal-sized piece of tape in the center of the flat piece of paper to keep the weights of both circles equal.
- Hold the circle in one hand and the cone, point side down, in the other, at the same height.
- Drop the cone and paper circle at the same time.
- Observe as they fall and strike the floor.

Results The paper cone hits the floor first.

Why? On Earth, falling objects pass through a layer of air called the **atmosphere**. As the objects fall, they collide with air molecules that exert an upward force on them. The amount of the uplifting force depends on the surface area of the object. The flat sheet of paper has a larger surface area and many molecules of air push upward on it causing it to fall more slowly than the cone. As the cone falls, it has less surface area so it breaks through the air molecules with fewer of them striking its surface, and thus falls faster.

191. Bigger

Purpose To demonstrate how a parachute works.

Materials scissors   small plastic garbage bag
              ruler   1 small washer
              string

Procedure
- Cut four separate strings about 20 inches (50 cm) long.
- Cut a 24-inch (60-cm) square from the plastic.
- Tie a string to each corner of the plastic square.
- Tie the four free ends of the strings together in a knot. Be sure the strings are all the same length.
- Use a string about 4 inches (10 cm) long to attach the washer to the knot in the parachute strings.
- Fold the plastic in half.
- Loosely wrap the string around the folded plastic.
- Throw the parachute up into the air.

Results The parachute opens and floats to the ground slowly.

Why? Objects push against air as the force of **gravity** causes them to fall. The upward push of the air molecules is called **air resistance**. Objects with a large surface, such as the parachute, have more air resistance. If the object has a large surface and a small **weight**, the upward push of air can decrease to the downward force, causing the object to float gently downward like a feather.

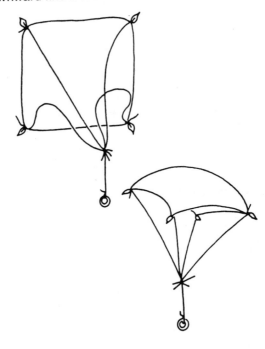

192. Floating Needle

Purpose To use a magnetic force to move a floating object.

Materials 2-quart (2-liter) glass bowl
              tap water
              scissors
              ruler
              sewing thread
              masking tape
              sewing needle
              bar magnet

Procedure
- Fill the bowl ¾ full with tap water.
- Cut two 12-inch (30-cm) pieces of thread.
- Tape both pieces of thread to one side of the bowl, about 1 inch (2.5 cm) apart.
- Stretch the thread across the bowl and lay the needle across both pieces.
- Slowly lower the thread until the needle rests on the water's surface.
- Gently move the thread from under the needle.
- Move the magnet near, but never touching, the floating needle.

Results The needle floats on the surface of the water and moves when the magnet moves.

Why? The surface of the water acts like a layer of thin skin due to the attraction of water molecules to each other. This thin layer is able to support the very light needle. The needle is attracted to the **magnetic field** of the magnet and is able to move across the surface in response.

193. Glider

Purpose To understand how magnetic trains move above their tracks.

Materials pencil
3-ounce (90-ml) paper cup
2 magnets with holes in the middle

Procedure
- Use the point of the pencil to make a hole in the bottom of the paper cup.
- Hollow the hole in the bottom of the cup with the pencil so that the pencil moves easily through the hole.
- Lay one magnet on a table.
- Slip the point of the pencil through the cup and then through the hole in the second magnet.
- Place the point of the pencil in the hole of the magnet on the table while holding up the other magnet and cup with your hand.
- Release the magnet and cup. NOTE: *If the magnets pull together, turn the magnet on the table upside down.*

Results The magnet and paper cup float above the magnet on the table.

Why? Every magnet has a north and a south pole. The opposite poles (north and south) are attracted to each other, and the like poles (north and north or south and south) **repel** (push away) each other. In this experiment, the magnets are positioned so that their poles repel, and one floats above the other. The cup represents a train with a magnet beneath it, and is suspended above the track with a repelling magnetic force.

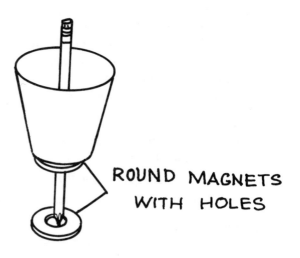

ROUND MAGNETS WITH HOLES

---

194. Magnetic Strength

Purpose To determine the strength of a magnetic field.

Materials masking tape
bar magnets, several different sizes
box of small paper clips

Procedure
- Tape the magnet to a table with part of the magnet extending over the edge of the table.
- Bend open the end of a paper clip and touch it to the bottom of the part of the magnet that extends over the table's edge.
- Add paper clips one at a time to the open clip until the clips pull loose from the magnet and fall.

Results The open paper clip hangs freely under the magnet. It continues to stay attached to the magnet as additional paper clips are added. The number of clips needed to cause the clips to fall will vary with different magnets.

Why? All magnets are surrounded by an area called a **magnetic field**, made up of invisible lines of force. A weak magnet has a weak magnetic field around it, so its effect on magnetic materials such as paper clips is small. The number of paper clips that your magnet is able to support depends on its magnetic strength. A strong magnet will support more paper clips.

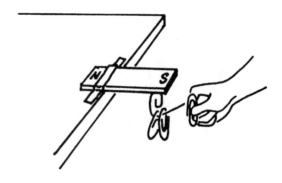

195. Puller

Purpose To demonstrate the force of attraction between charged particles.

Materials modeling clay
coin
toothpick
balloon, small enough to hold in your hand

Procedure
- Press a walnut-sized piece of clay onto a table.
- Push the edge of the coin into the clay so that the coin stands upright.
- Balance the toothpick across the top edge of the standing coin.
- Charge the balloon by rubbing it on your hair or a wool scarf about 10 times. Your hair must be clean, dry, and oil-free.
- Hold the charged balloon near, but not touching, the toothpick.
- Watch the toothpick for any movement.

Results The toothpick turns and falls off the edge of the coin.

Why? The toothpick, balloon, and hair are all examples of matter, and all matter is made of minute units called **atoms**. Atoms have positively charged **protons** in their **nucleus** (center of an atom) and negatively charged **electrons** spinning around the nucleus. The balloon becomes negatively charged on the side that is rubbed on your hair because the electrons are rubbed off the hair and collect on the balloon. This build-up of electrical charges that remain in one place is called **static electricity**. The negatively charged balloon attracts the positive part of the toothpick. This attraction is strong enough to pull the wooden stick off the coin.

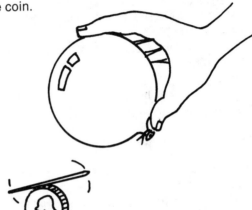

196. Swinger

Purpose To determine if the north pole of a magnet always points to the Earth's magnetic north pole.

Materials scissors
ruler
sewing thread
small paper clip
cellophane tape
book
magnet
compass

Procedure
- Cut a 12-inch (30-cm) piece of thread.
- Attach one end of the thread to the center of the paper clip with a very small piece of tape.
- Tie the other end of the thread to one end of the ruler.
- Set the book on the edge of a table and place the other end of the ruler under the book so that the ruler hangs over the edge of the table.
- Place the paper clip on the magnet.
- Remove the clip from the magnet and allow it to swing freely from the string.
- Observe the direction toward which the end of the paper clip points.
- Use the compass to determine what direction that is.
- Move the ruler to different positions and observe the direction the paper clip points each time.

Results One end of the paper clip points south and the other points north. Moving the ruler does not effect the direction that the paper clip points.

Why? A **magnetic field** surrounds the Earth. Any suspended magnet, such as the magnetized paper clip, will align itself with this magnetic field. The end of the hanging magnet pointing toward the Earth's north magnetic pole is called the north pole, and the end of the magnet pointing toward the Earth's south magnetic pole is called the south pole.

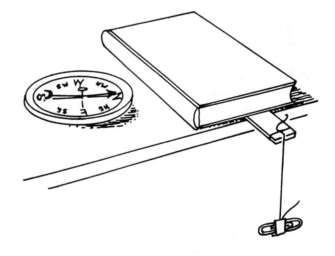

197. Fly Away

Purpose To demonstrate the effect of static electricity.

Materials   scissors
ruler
newspaper

Procedure

NOTE: *This experiment works best when the air is dry and cool.*

- Cut two strips of newspaper 1-inch × 12-inches (1.25-cm × 30-cm).
- Hold the two strips of paper together at one end.
- Put the middle finger of your other hand between the strips.
- Squeeze the papers lightly between your fingers and quickly pull your hand down the strips.

Results The paper strips fly apart.

Why? All materials are made up of atoms that have positively charged **protons** in their nucleus and negatively charged **electrons** spinning around the nucleus. When two different substances, such as your hand and the paper, are rubbed together, electrons leave the surface of one material and collect on the surface of the other material. The electrons have a negative charge, so one material develops a negative charge and the other a positive charge. This collection of electric charges that remain stationary in one place is called **static electricity**. Materials with like charges **repel** each other. Thus, the paper pieces fly apart because they have similar charges.

---

198. Glow

Purpose To determine how a fluorescent tube works.

Materials   balloon   paper towel
liquid soap   adult helper
fluorescent tube

Procedure

- Inflate and tie the balloon.
- Ask an adult to wash the outside of the fluorescent tube and thoroughly dry it with a paper towel.
- In a dark room, place one end of the tube against the floor. Ask your adult helper to assist in supporting the tube.
- Hold the tube upright and quickly rub the balloon up and down the outside of it.
CAUTION: *Care should be taken not to press too hard or the tube might break.*

Results The fluorescent tube starts to glow and the light moves with the movement of the balloon.

Why? Rubbing the tube results in a build-up of static charges on the outside of the glass. This outside charge attracts charged particles inside the tube. The phosphor powder coating the inside of the tube gives off light when struck by these charged particles.

199. Tinkle

Purpose To demonstrate the effect of static electricity.

Materials scissors
aluminum foil
comb

Procedure
- Cut 10 tiny pieces of aluminum foil and lay them on a table.
- Quickly move the comb through your hair. Your hair must be clean, dry, and oil-free.
- Hold the teeth of the comb above the foil pieces. Do not touch the aluminum.

Results The aluminum foil pieces move toward the comb. The metal actually moves through the air to reach the comb.

Why? Aluminum foil is made of atoms, which are composed of positive parts called **protons** and negative parts called **electrons**. The protons are in the center of the atom (the **nucleus**) and the electrons spin around the outside of the nucleus. The comb rubs electrons off your hair and becomes negatively charged. Like charges **repel** each other and unlike charges attract. As the negatively charged comb approaches the metal pieces, the negative electrons in the metal move away from the comb, leaving more positive charges on the surface of the metal. The attraction between the negatively charged comb and the positive area on the metal is strong enough to overcome the downward pull of **gravity**, and the metal pieces move through the air to stick to the comb.

200. Galvanometer

Purpose To construct a galvanometer.

Materials inexpensive compass
cardboard box to fit the compass
thin, insulated wire, 22 gauge
D-cell battery
adult helper

Procedure
- Construct a galvanometer by following these steps:
  Place the compass in the box.
  Wind the wire around the box, about 50 times, leaving about 12 inches (30 cm) free on both ends.
  Ask an adult helper to scrape about 2 inches (10 cm) of the insulation from the ends of the wires.
- Turn the galvanometer so that the compass needle and wire wrapped around the box both point in a north-to-south direction.
- Touch one end of the wire to the top of the battery and the other end of the wire to the bottom.
- Watch the compass needle as you hold one wire against the end of the battery and alternately touch the other wire to the battery and remove it several times.
- Disconnect the wires from the battery and keep the galvanometer for Experiment 201.

Results The needle on the compass moves away from, and then returns to, its north-to-south direction when the wire is touched to and then removed from the battery.

Why? The **galvanometer** is an instrument used to detect **electric current** (a flow of electric charges from one place to the other). Electric charges move from the battery through the wire, and back to the battery. An electric current produces a **magnetic field**. Since the wire is turned in a north-to-south direction, the movement of the current through the wire produces a magnetic field pointing east and west. The needle of the compass will be pulled toward this magnetic field, thus indicating that an electric current is flowing through the wire. The larger the current through the wire, the stronger the magnetic field that is produced.

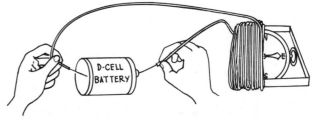

201. Battery

Purpose To produce an electric current.

Materials aluminum-foil baking cup
tap water
2 teaspoons (10 ml) of table salt
spoon
galvanometer (from Experiment 200)
paper clip
metal washer

Procedure

- Fill the aluminum-foil baking cup ¾ full with water.
- Add the salt to the water and stir.
- Connect one end of the wire to the cup with a paper clip.
- Turn the galvanometer so that the compass needle is parallel with the wire wrapped around the box.
- Press the other end of the wire against the washer and dip it into the salt solution close to, but not touching, the paper clip.
- Alternately dip and raise the washer from the solution as you watch the compass needle.

Results The needle on the compass moves. NOTE: Add more salt if the needle does not move.

Why? The Italian physicist Alessandro Volta (1745–1827) discovered that electricity could be produced by separating two different metals by an electrical conducting liquid, such as salt water. The flow of current in this experiment is very small, but it is enough to move the needle on the homemade **galvanometer**.

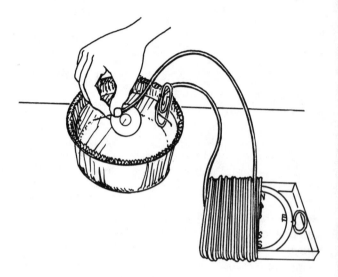

Glossary

Absorb: Take in or swallow up.

Acid: A chemical that tastes sour; the opposite of a base; neutralizes bases.

Air Resistance: The push of air against moving objects; upward push on falling objects.

Amplitude: The height of movement, such as a sound wave; loud sounds have a high amplitude.

Anemometer: An instrument that shows how fast wind blows.

Antifreeze: A substance that, when added to a liquid, causes the liquid to freeze at a lower temperature.

Atmosphere: Mass of gas surrounding the Earth or any other celestial body.

Atmospheric Pressure: The weight of the atmosphere against the earth's surface.

Atoms: Minute units of matter having protons and neutrons in its nucleus and electrons spinning outside the nucleus.

Bacteria: Microscopic living things. They are more like plants than animals; some of the simplest forms of life.

Ball Bearings: Spheres placed between a wheel and its axle to reduce friction.

Barycenter: Center of gravity point between the Earth-Moon system. Point at which this system moves around the Sun.

Base: A chemical that is the opposite of an acid; tastes bitter; neutralizes acids; turns turmeric paper red, and turns phenolphthalein bright pink.

Bernoulli's Principle: A principle stating that faster moving fluids, such as air, exert less pressure than slower moving fluids.

Buoyant Force: The upward force that a liquid exerts on an object in it. The force is equal to the weight of the liquid that is pushed aside when the object is submersed in the liquid.

Caliche: (ka lee' chee) Deposits of limestone (calcium carbonate) near or on the surface of the ground.

Center of Gravity: The point on an object where it can be balanced; point where the weight of an object appears to be located.

Centripetal Force: A force that tends to move a rotating object toward the center of rotation.

Cephids: Variable stars that give off different amounts of light due to a change in temperature; stars that have regular pulsations.

Chlorophyll: The green pigment that plants use in the energy reaction called photosynthesis.

Clouds: Mass of tiny drops of liquid water in the sky.

Color Contrast: How well the color of something stands out against its background.

Comet: A cloud of frozen gases, ice, dust, and rock orbiting the Sun; usually has a long cloudy tail.

Concave Lens: A lens that curves inward; objects appear smaller when viewed through this lens.

Concentrated: Pure, not diluted with other materials.

Condense: Change from gas phase to liquid phase.

Conductor: A material that allows heat to move through it.

Conservation of Energy: Energy, such as heat, cannot be made or destroyed. Heat energy lost by one substance is gained by another substance.

Constellation: A group of stars that, viewed from the Earth, form the outline of an object or figure.

Contracts: Moves closer together.

Convection Currents: Movement of air or liquids due to differences in temperature.

Convex Lens: A lens that curves outward; magnifying lens.

Cotyledon: Food source for plant embryo (baby plant).

Craters: Holes, such as those on the moon's surface.

Crest: The top part of a transverse wave.

Decompose: To rot; to break into simpler parts.

Deductive Reasoning: A type of reasoning in which a conclusion is formed from the experimental results.

Density: The scientific way of comparing the "heaviness" of materials. It is a measurement of the mass of a specific volume.

Dermis: The inner layer of skin.

Dew: Moisture condensed from the air.

Dew Point: Temperature at which water vapor in the air condenses.

Dike: Rock structure formed when magma fills and hardens in a vertical crack in rock.

Dilute: To lessen the strength by mixing with another material, usually water.

Dissolve: To break apart into smaller and smaller particles; in time particles spread out evenly through a dissolving medium.

Electric Current: A flow of electric charges from one place to the other.

Electromagnetic Spectrum: A group of energy waves traveling at the speed of light and do not require the presence of matter.

Electron: Negative particle that spins around the nucleus or core of an atom.

Epicotyl: The part of a plant embryo (baby plant) that develops into leaves.

Epidermis: Outer layer of skin.

Evaporation: Process by which a liquid changes to a gas by increasing the heat content of the liquid.

Evaporation Rate: Speed that a liquid, such as water, evaporates.

Expand: Moves farther apart.

Fossil: Any impression or trace of organisms from past geologic times.

Frequency: The number of vibrations per second.

Friction: A force that tends to stop objects sliding past each other; produces heat energy.

Frost: Feathery ice crystals formed when water vapor sublimes, changes from a gas directly to a solid.

Fungus: An organism that has both plant and animal characteristics. Fungi means food-robbing.

Galaxy: A large group of stars, such as the Milky Way galaxy.

Galvanometer: Instrument used to detect a small electric current.

Gears: Wheels with teeth around the outer rim that mesh with other such wheels.

Geostationary Operational Environmental Satellite (GOES):   A satellite that has a period of rotation of 24 hours, thus appearing to remain stationary above one point on the Earth.

Glaciers: Large masses of ice in motion.

Gravity: The force that pulls celestial bodies toward each other; force that pulls everything on Earth toward the ground.

Gyroscope: A disk or wheel that spins rapidly about its axis. When spinning, its axis tends to remain pointing in the same direction.

Hilum: Scar on a bean showing where the bean was attached to the pod wall.

Humidity: The amount of water in air.

Hypocotyl: Part of a plant embryo (baby plant) that develops into the stem.

Inclined Plane: A flat, tilted surface used as a ramp.

Indicator: A chemical that changes color in acids and/or bases.

Inertia: The resistance that an object has to having its motion changed. Objects that are stationary continue to be at rest, while objects in motion continue to move in a straight line due to their inertia. Stationary objects move and moving objects stop only when some outside force acts on them.

Infrared Light: Heat waves; electromagnetic waves given off by all objects, the amount depends on their temperature with hot objects emitting the most; warming solar rays.

Insulator: Materials that help prevent temperature changes.

Kinetic Energy: Energy of motion.

Laccolith: Dome-shaped hardened magma formed between rock layers.

Larynx: Short passage connecting the throat with lower airways; called the voice box.

Lichen: A plant with no roots, leaves, or flowers. It is not a single plant but is actually two plants—a fungus and an algae—growing together.

Lift: The upward push on the underside of the wings of birds or airplanes due to the difference in the speed of airflow across the top and bottom of the wings.

Luciferin: A chemical that some organisms have that gives off light when combined with oxygen.

Luminous Body: Object that gives off its own light.

Magma: Liquid rock beneath the Earth's surface.

Magnetic Field: Area around a magnet in which the force of the magnet affects the movement of other magnetic objects.

Magnetite: An iron ore mass, strongly attracted by a magnet.

Magnitude of Stars: A measure of a star's brightness as seen from Earth; degree of brightness.

Mass: The amount of material an object contains.

Matter: The substance things are made of. Matter takes up space and has inertia or mass.

Mechanical Energy: Energy in moving objects.

Meteor: Meteoroids that burn in the Earth's atmosphere.

Meteorite: A stony or metallic object from space that reaches the surface of a celestial body.

Meteoroid: Variable-sized pieces of material floating in space.

Micropyle: A small opening through which a pollen grain enters a seed.

Mold: A form of fungus.

Nebula: A vast cloud of dust and gas in space.

Neutralization: A process in which an acidic and basic solution are brought to a neutral state, that is neither acidic nor basic.

Newton's Third Law of Motion: For every action, there is an equal and opposite reaction.

Nucleus: Center of an atom; contains positively charged protons and neutrally charged neutrons.

Opaque: A material that light rays cannot pass through.

Optical Illusion: Visual trickery; a false mental image or concept.

Osmosis: The movement of water through a cell membrane; movement is toward an area with the lesser amount of water.

Persistence of Vision: The retention of an image by the brain for a fraction of a second after the object is no longer visible.

Phenolphthalein: An indicator for a base.

Photosynthesis: Energy-producing reaction in plants. It uses carbon dioxide, water, and sunlight to produce oxygen, glucose, and energy; glucose molecules combine to form starch and cellulose.

Pitch: The number of vibrations that reach the ear in one second. The pitch of sound increases as the vibrations increase.

Placer Ore: Metal particles that form a layer over rock.

Polaris: North star; star that the Earth's imaginary axis points to.

Pollutant: A substance that is harmful to living organisms.

Potential Energy: Stored energy due to position. The higher the object, the more potential energy it has.

Predator: Any animal that preys on another animal.

Prism: A transparent object, usually made of glass, that breaks the white light of the Sun into its separate colors of red, orange, yellow, green, blue, indigo, and violet; most common is a triangular prism, which looks like a wedge.

Propagate: To cause to reproduce; to cause to multiply from parent stock.

Proton: Positively charged particle in the nucleus of an atom.

Psychrometer: Instrument used to measure relative humidity.

Pupil: Opening in the front of the eye through which light passes.

Radiation: A process by which energy such as heat is transferred; does not require the presence of matter; name given to energy waves that make up the electromagnetic spectrum.

Radicle: The part of a plant embryo (baby plant) that develops into roots.

Refraction: The change of speed of light as it moves out of one material and into another; bending of light waves.

Regelation: The melting of a substance due to pressure and its refreezing when the pressure is released.

Relative humidity: Amount of water vapor in air compared to the amount that the air can hold at that temperature.

Repel: To push away from.

Resolution: The measurement of the ability to see details.

Retina: The light sensitive layer on the back of the eyeball where images are focused.

Rotation: Turning of an object about its own axis.

Satellite: A small object that circles a larger body.

Saturated Solution: The state that exists when no additional solute can dissolve in a solvent at a specific temperature.

Seed Coat: Protective covering on a seed.

Semi-permeable Membrane: A material that allows different-sized materials to pass through it.

Sill: A rock structure formed when magma squeezes in and hardens between sedimentary rock layers.

Soap Scum: A slimy solid formed when minerals in hard water react with soap.

Solar Eclipse: The blocking of some of the sunlight when a body comes between the Sun and the observer; commonly when the Moon comes between the Sun and the Earth; most frequent type of eclipse, but seen by the least number of people.

Solute: Dissolving material; material that dissolves in a solvent.

Solvent: Dissolving medium; the material that a solute dissolves in.

Static Electricity: The build-up of electrical charges, positive or negative, which remains in one place; static means stationary.

Sublimes: Changes directly from a gas to a solid without forming a liquid.

Surface Current: Horizontal movement of water on the surface of a body of water.

Suspension: A mixture containing particles suspended in a liquid or gas that usually settles on standing.

Tendon: Strong bands of tissue that attaches muscle to bone.

Tension: A stretching or pulling force.

Translucent: A material that allows some light to pass through, but changes the direction of the light rays.

Transparent: A material that allows light rays to pass straight through.

Transverse Waves: Waves that move up and down like water waves.

Trough: The bottom part of a transverse wave.

Tuber: An underground plant stem; potato.

Vibration: The back-and-forth movement of materials.

Viscosity: The measurement of the thickness of a fluid or its resistance to flowing.

Vocal Cord: Two folds of tissue stretched across the larynx; air vibrates the cords, creating the sound of the voice.

Weathering: The breaking and wearing away of rocks and other land features.

Wedge: A solid triangular material used to raise, pry open, or split apart a material.

Weight: Downward (toward the Earth's surface) force due to gravity. Depends on mass; objects with more mass have more weight.

Xylem: Tiny tubes in the stalk of a plant stem; transports water and minerals from the roots to the rest of the plant.

Index

More Exciting and Fun Activity Books from Janice VanCleave . . .

**Available from your local bookstore
or simply use the order form below.**

Mail to: Jennifer Bergman, John Wiley and Sons, Inc.,
605 Third Avenue, New York, New York, 10158

To Order
by Phone:

Call
1-800-225-5945

Title	ISBN	Price
__ ANIMALS	55052-3	$9.95
__ EARTHQUAKES	57107-5	$9.95
__ ELECTRICITY	31010-7	$9.95
__ GRAVITY	55050-7	$9.95
__ MACHINES	57108-3	$9.95
__ MAGNETS	57106-7	$9.95
__ MICROSCOPES	58956-X	$9.95
__ MOLECULES	55054-X	$9.95
__ VOLCANOES	30811-0	$9.95
__ ASTRONOMY	53573-7	$10.95
__ BIOLOGY	50381-9	$10.95
__ CHEMISTRY	62085-8	$10.95
__ DINOSAURS	30812-9	$10.95
__ EARTH SCIENCE	53010-7	$10.95
__ GEOGRAPHY	59842-9	$10.95
__ GEOMETRY	31141-3	$10.95
__ MATH	54265-2	$10.95
__ PHYSICS	52505-7	$10.95
__ 200 GOOEY, SLIPPERY, SLIMY, WEIRD, & FUN		
EXPERIMENTS	57921-1	$12.95
__ 201 AWESOME, MAGICAL, BIZARRE, INCREDIBLE		
EXPERIMENTS	31011-5	$12.95

Total:_____

Wiley pays postage & handling for prepaid orders
[ ] Check/Money order enclosed
[ ] Charge my: [ ]VISA   [ ]MASTERCARD   [ ]AMEX   [ ]DISCOVER
Card #:_____ Expiration Date:_____/_____
NAME:_____
ADDRESS:_____
CITY/STATE/ZIP:_____
SIGNATURE:_____
(Order not valid unless signed)

 **WILEY**
Publishers Since 1807